THE WHITE HOUSE
Cornerstone of a Nation

Cross Section of the White House from the South

Ground Floor
1. East Wing corridor
2. Library
3. Vermeil Room
4. China Room
5. Diplomatic Reception Room
6. Map Room

State Floor
7. East Room
8. Green Room
9. Blue Room
10. South Portico
11. Red Room
12. State Dining Room
13. Family Dining Room
14. Cross Hall
15. Entrance Hall

Family Quarters
16. East lunette window
17. Truman balcony

Third Floor
18. Solarium

The White House, 1877.

JUDITH ST. GEORGE

THE WHITE HOUSE

Cornerstone of a Nation

ILLUSTRATED WITH PHOTOGRAPHS

G. P. PUTNAM'S SONS, NEW YORK

Copyright © 1990 by Judith St. George
G. P. Putnam's Sons, a division of
The Putnam & Grosset Book Group,
200 Madison Avenue, New York, NY 10016.
Published simultaneously in Canada.
Printed in the United States of America.
Book design by Christy Hale.
The text was set in Century Schoolbook.
Library of Congress Cataloging-in-Publication Data
St. George, Judith. The White House :
cornerstone of a nation / Judith St. George ;
illustrated with photographs.
p. cm. Includes bibliographical references.
Summary: Discusses some of the changes and
the events occuring over two centuries
in the building that represents the power and
majesty of the presidency.
ISBN 0-399-22186-7
1. White House (Washington D.C.)—Juvenile literature.
2. Presidents—United States—History—Juvenile literature.
3. Washington (D.C.)—Buildings, structures, etc.—Juvenile
literature. [1. White House (Washington D.C.)
2. Presidents—History.] I. Title.
F204.W5S7 1990 975.3—dc20 89-27005 CIP AC
10 9 8 7 6 5 4 3 2 1
First Impression

For my friends Sally and Tim

CONTENTS

INTRODUCTION

President Calvin Coolidge and a friend were returning to the White House after a walk when the friend jokingly asked, "I wonder who lives there."

"Nobody," President Coolidge replied. "They just come and go."

President Coolidge's wry comment was only partly true.

It is certainly true that Presidents come and go, some as swiftly as William Henry Harrison, who died within a month of becoming President, or as long as Franklin Delano Roosevelt, who occupied the White House for more than twelve years. But it is also true that every American President since 1792 has left his imprint on the White House, whether it was as major as President George Washington's architectural changes or as minor as the addition of President Ulysses S. Grant's billiards room.

More than any one administration, however, the social, economic and political conditions in the country have had an even greater impact on how the White House has developed and changed. Much like a mirror, the White House has reflected the country's wars, depressions, tragedies and good times.

This book is not intended to be a definitive history of the White House or the nation. Rather it is a personal selection of those times that have most dramatically influenced the building that for two centuries has represented the power and majesty of the presidency, the White House.

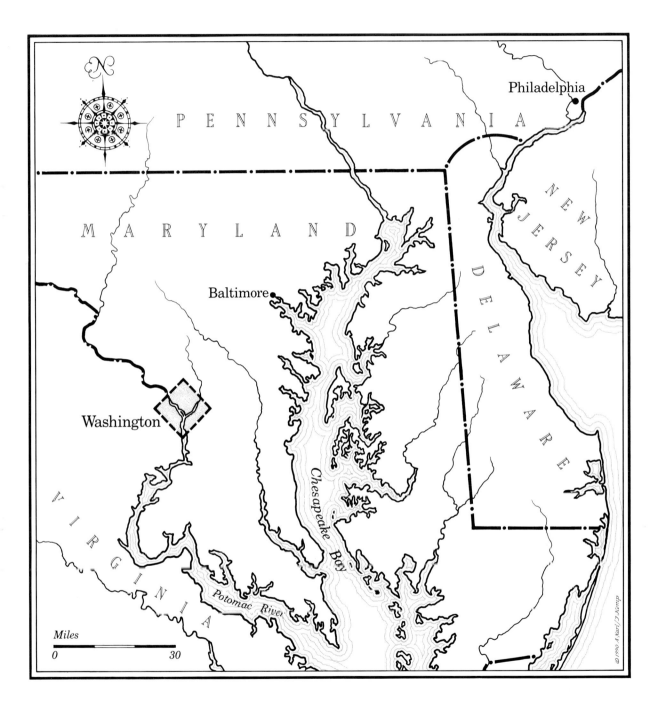

1 THE WHITE HOUSE BEGUN

THE THREE MEN SPENT A GOOD DEAL of time that June afternoon in 1791 looking over the hilly tract of farmland and woods above the Potomac River. The architect in the group pointed out where he wanted the building to be located, but the tall, distinguished-looking gentleman who spoke with obvious authority had another idea. He preferred a site that would be "more westerly for the advantage of higher ground" so that the building would have a grander setting while still keeping its fine view of the Potomac River.

That night the President wrote in his diary, "Tuesday—28th . . . I went out with Maj^{rs} L'Enfant and Ellicott to take a more perfect view of the ground, in order to decide finally on the spots on which to place the public buildings." The momentous decision had been made. President George Washington, architect Pierre Charles L'Enfant and surveyor Andrew Ellicott had selected the site for the future home of Presidents in the wilderness that would one day become the capital of the United States.

Map of the Washington area, 1792.

To satisfy the North, the South and President Washington too, Secretary of State Thomas Jefferson, Secretary of the Treasury Alexander Hamilton and Congressman James Madison had arrived at a compromise that would place the new capital in the center of the country near Georgetown, Maryland. The land, which included parts of both Maryland and Virginia, would cover an area "not exceeding ten miles square, to be located . . . on the river Potomac." The three commissioners, who had been appointed by President Washington to supervise the project, wrote, "We have agreed that the Federal district shall be called the 'Territory of Columbia' and the Federal city the 'City of Washington.'"

The Residence Act of 1790, which had made President Washington responsible for setting up the federal capital, had also set "the first Monday in December, 1800" as the deadline for finishing both the President's house and the Capitol building for Congress. Washington, who had been inaugurated President in 1789 and was living in the temporary capital of Philadelphia, knew that by 1800 he would no longer be in office. Nevertheless, he had very definite ideas about what he wanted and what he didn't want in the way of a house that would symbolize the presidency to the American people.

By March 1791 Washington had selected Pierre Charles L'Enfant to design the new city and its government buildings, describing the French architect as "better qualified than any one who [has] come within my knowledge in this country, or indeed, in any other . . ." During 1791 and 1792, L'Enfant, who had lived at the French court, discussed with Washington his plans that would transform the Territory of Columbia's ten square miles of marsh, forests and farmlands into a handsomely laid-out city of wide streets and impressive stone buildings. And Washington was well pleased with L'Enfant's design for the President's Palace that

14

In 1796 Edward Savage paints President George Washington, his wife, Martha, and her two grandchildren studying a map of the new City of Washington.

would measure approximately 700 feet by 200 feet, a palace indeed!

But right from the beginning, L'Enfant refused to work with anyone except the President, certainly not with Secretary of State Thomas Jefferson, who was in charge of the project, or with the three commissioners. As for American politics, L'Enfant didn't understand or care about them.

Washington, on the other hand, was very much aware that he had to work within the political system, a system that much to his dismay, had increasingly split into two quarreling political parties. The Federalist Party favored a strong central government and leadership by an educated, wealthy ruling class. (George Washington was basically a Federalist.) The Antifederalist Party opposed a strong central government, believing that the people should govern themselves in a nation made up of small farms with only a few cities. (Thomas Jefferson was an Antifederalist.) The Antifederalists, especially Jefferson, viewed L'Enfant's plan for the federal capital with its giant government buildings, monuments, plazas, fountains, and most especially, its Presidential Palace, as much too "royal."

Although New York and Philadelphia had already started to build presidential mansions in the hopes that the City of Washington would never be finished, L'Enfant, who by late 1791 had begun to excavate the foundation and cellar, refused to hurry or take advice from anyone. Washington, who could be practical as well as visionary, began to realize that his dream of a federal city might never come to pass if he didn't get rid of the arrogant L'Enfant. "I am instructed by the President to inform you that . . . your services must be at an end," a doubtlessly well-pleased Jefferson wrote to L'Enfant on February 27, 1792.

Washington may have given up on plans for a grand palace, but he never gave up on L'Enfant's plans for the federal city, the center of which would one day be laid out much as L'Enfant had designed

Although the 1795 map of the City of Washington is engraved from L'Enfant's original plan, his name appears nowhere on it.

Detail of map—The White House, the Mall and the Capitol Building remain today where L'Enfant originally located them.

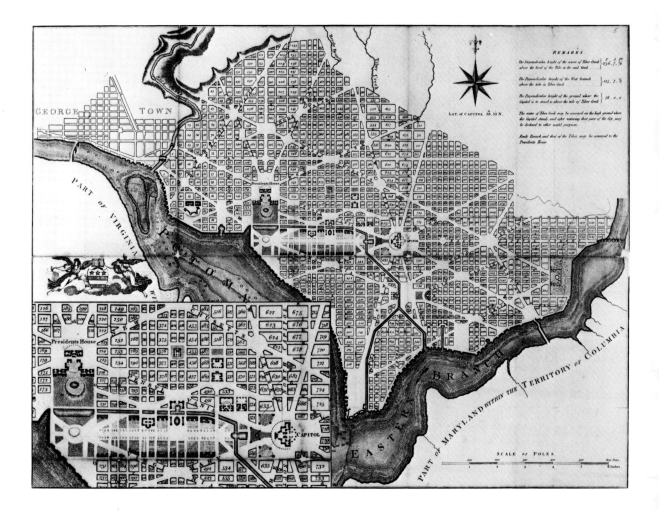

it. ". . . the public buildings in size, form and elegance should look beyond the present day," Washington wrote to the three commissioners, adding, "For the Presidents House, I would design a building which should also look forward."

Anxious for the project to get underway, Washington went along with Jefferson's suggestion to hold a competition for the best design for the Capitol building and for what was now to be called the President's House. On March 14, 1792, newspapers ran an advertisement offering either a $500 prize or a gold medal for "the most approved plan for a President's house." Jefferson may have written the advertisement, and the commissioners may have signed it, but it was President Washington who made the final choice. Out of nine entries, the winner was James Hoban, an Irish architect who had designed a handsome three-story stone building. (One of the entries, signed A.Z., is believed to have been submitted by Jefferson.)

On July 18, 1792, the commissioners wrote that the President had approved a plan for the mansion " which we think convenient, elegant, and within a moderate expence." Winning plans or not, Washington was so certain that Hoban's design wouldn't meet the needs of future Presidents, he insisted that the building be enlarged by one-fifth and that the exterior stone carvings be made more elaborate. Because his changes turned out to be so expensive, Washington agreed to eliminate the entire third floor to satisfy the worried commissioners. To save even more money, the commissioners, on their own, ordered that the building be constructed of

James Hoban's final design for the White House, which has eliminated the third floor, reveals triangles alternating with arches over the State Floor windows.

brick covered over by stone rather than of solid stone as the original plans had called for. (The final cost was somewhere around $300,000.)

On August 2, 1792, Washington, Hoban and the three commissioners traveled to the property where Washington, who had once been a surveyor, studied the plans and paced out the site. The commissioners later reported that the exact location of the building gave Washington "considerable Trouble and difficulty to fix his mind." At last he made his decision. The front door would be *here*. Because Hoban's house, although the largest in the nation, would be so much smaller than the one L'Enfant had designed, it was no longer on a direct line, or axis, with the Capitol building 1.2 miles away at the other end of Pennsylvania Avenue.

Hoban's plans called for entering the thirty-six-room house by the north front door into a wide Entrance Hall that had a service staircase to the left and a small office to the right. Four columns beneath three arches separated the Entrance Hall from the long Cross, or Transverse, Hall that ran lengthwise through the center of the house. Opening off the Cross Hall were three State Rooms in a row, all facing to the south, or rear of the house, the Green Room to the left, the oval Blue Room in the center directly opposite the front door and the Red Room to the right. The Blue Room, which over the years has been called the Oval Drawing Room, the Blue Elliptical Saloon, the Oval Parlor or the Large Oval Room, was shaped like an egg that extended out from the building in a semicircle. There was an identical oval room above the Blue Room on the second floor and below in the basement, the three rooms making a dramatic focus for each floor.

To the left, at the far end of the Cross Hall, was the enormous East Room, measuring 80 feet long by 40 feet wide. At the opposite end of the Cross Hall was the grand stairway that separated the State Dining Room and the Family Dining Room (not considered a State Room). The five State Rooms, which all opened onto one another, were 18 feet high, with the East Room a handsome 22 feet high.

In September 1792, Hoban, who was general supervisor as well

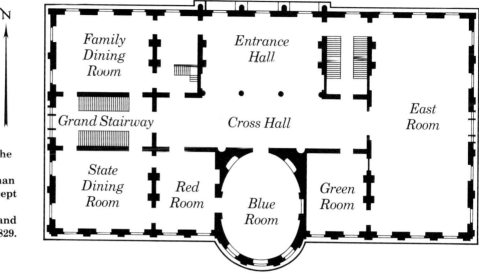

Family Dining Room

Entrance Hall

Grand Stairway

Cross Hall

East Room

State Dining Room

Red Room

Blue Room

Green Room

N

Hoban's floor plan of the White House is unchanged for more than one hundred years except for the addition of the South Portico in 1824 and the North Portico in 1829.

as architect, had his men start on the foundation of the house where L'Enfant had already begun excavation. The workers laid foundation stones on top of a thick bed of rough and broken stones and then laid rectangular cut-stone blocks for the basement on top of the foundation stones.

The following month, those men most concerned with the President's House, except for Washington and Jefferson, marched from nearby Georgetown to the rear southwest corner of the building site to lay the cornerstone. After "an oration well adapted to the occasion," Scotsman Collen Williamson, master stonemason in charge of all stonework, spread mortar on a foundation stone, pressed a brass plate into the mortar, and then tamped the cornerstone on top of the plate. "This first stone of the President's House was laid the 13th day of October 1792, and in the seventeenth year of the independence of the United States of America," was engraved on the plate, followed by the names of the President, the three commissioners, the architect and the master mason.

In 1790, when Congress had set a deadline of December 1800 for moving the capital from Philadelphia to the City of Washington, ten years had seemed like more than enough time to finish the project. But finding skilled workers, especially stonecutters, wasn't easy, and although the building trade was booming, few workers wanted to leave good jobs and move to the raw little City of Washington where slave labor kept wages low. In desperation, the commissioners began hiring skilled stonecutters from Scotland, although it wasn't until 1794 that six Scottish stonecutters were actually on the job.

All the stone for the President's House was arkose sandstone that came from the Aquia Creek quarry in Virginia, forty miles away. Because the rather soft sandstone absorbs water and has a tendency to crack in freezing weather, it has to be sealed, either by painting or whitewashing. When the stone is dry, it appears sand-colored with a rosy tint, but when it is wet, it turns a dull gray.

Since the stone walls were first whitewashed in 1797, they have been painted or whitewashed some twenty-eight times, building up so many layers of paint, much of the fine detail of the elegant stone carvings has almost been hidden. In 1980, after three years of research and testing, work was started on removing these layers of

The bare stone wall from which the paint has been removed is in sharp contrast to the adjoining repainted wall, August 1989.

paint down to bare stone and repainting the mansion at a cost of approximately $3,000,000. The newly cleaned walls have not only revealed the delicate beauty of the carvings, but also the ornamental parallel lines in the basement walls that were cut with a special tool called a tooth chisel.

At the Aquia Creek quarry, the stones were split off from the huge natural bed of stone, roughly cut to the desired size and numbered as to where Collen Williamson planned to set them in the building. Boats then transported the rough-cut stone down Aquia Creek to the Potomac River and from there to the building site.

All stonecutting was done in huge sheds constructed in the north yard of the President's House where the stonecutters carefully followed Williamson's large-scale drawings of where each stone should be placed. After the stones were finished, or smoothed, they were rubbed with sand to polish them and then numbered according to the order in which they would be set in the walls. Although a thin layer of mortar was used to set the finished stones, they fit one another so perfectly, mortar wasn't really needed. If the stonecutter was being paid by the job, he identified his work by chiseling his personal mark in the last stone set.

In 1795 the ornamental stone carvings of classical chains and

The original stone carvings over the north door of the White House are among the most beautiful in the country.

elaborate garlands of flowers and leaves over the front door was begun, as well as carvings on the moldings, chimneys, cornices, tops of the columns and around the windows and windowsills. Again following the master stonemason's large-scale drawings, the carvers used a hammer and chisel to block out the rough shapes before penciling the exact design on the stone, which they then painstakingly chiseled out in detail.

Because the clay-and-sand soil at the President's House was ideal for making bricks, brickwork was done right on the property. When the commissioners ordered that brick be used for the inner shells of all the city's public buildings, the master brickmaker suddenly found himself responsible for turning out thousands of bricks a day.

Pits were dug in the north yard where the clay, water and sand were combined, with the resulting mixture then solidly packed in wooden molds. After the raw bricks were taken out of the molds, they were dried, either in the sun or in drying sheds until they were firm enough to stack for firing, or baking, in ovens called kilns. Because the bricks were to be used for interior walls, they were fired at a lower temperature than if they had been for exterior walls, resulting in a rather soft pinkish brick.

Lumber for future floors, doors, paneling, moldings and the interior framing was readily available in the area and Hoban ordered yellow and white pine, white oak and poplar from local landowners, including property in Virginia owned by Washington.

By the time work closed down in the fall of 1793 for the winter, the basement story was finished, with walls that were 13 feet high and more than 3 feet thick. At last the public could see the actual size of the house, 168 feet long east to west and 85 feet wide north to south. Because Washington had wanted the house to command an important setting, it was set on a steep hillside that sloped down to the Potomac River on the south so that the basement on the north, or front side, was at ground level, while the basement on the south side was a full story above ground level. In order for the north basement to be above ground level too, Hoban excavated the area across the front of the house.

At the same time that the basement walls were going up, work was going on inside the basement. Fortunately, all of the interior piers, or supports, for the arched ceiling of the basement, called groin vaulting, as well as some of the arches that would eventually support the weight of the house, had already been constructed of solid stone before the commissioners made the decision to build the house of brick faced with stone.

Because the interior brick walls went up first, they were always a little higher than the outer stone walls. As the brick and stone walls continued to rise during 1794 and 1795, wooden scaffolding totally encircled the house, while the front yard and what is now Lafayette Park across Pennsylvania Avenue, became a hodgepodge of workers' huts, sheds, privies, pits, kilns, a cookhouse, eating hall, carpenter shop, brickyard, stoneyard and sawmill, not to mention rubble, trash and mud.

Considering that the United States was only twenty years old, it wasn't surprising that half of the laborers and almost all of the skilled workers were foreigners. At daybreak, except on Sundays, the work force assembled for roll call, followed by a free breakfast of cornbread and a pound of meat. During the summer the men working on the high scaffolding were given a pint of whiskey or rum a day with an extra half-pint when the weather was especially hot in the belief that liquor built strong bodies.

As Washington began his last year as President in 1796, the Antifederalists, now called Democratic-Republicans, sensing that Washington's power was fading, once more criticized the "royal" grandeur of what they were again calling "the President's Palace." Unhappy as Washington was over the bitter friction between the Democratic-Republicans and the Federalists, he was determined that both the President's House and the Capitol building should be far enough along so that no matter who followed him as the next President, nothing could stop completion of the buildings.

Raising a battle cry of hurry-hurry-hurry that would be repeated by every future President faced with a White House deadline, Washington wrote the commissioners in May 1796, "The year 1800 is approaching by hasty strides; The friends of the City are extremely anxious to see the public works keep equal pace there-with." But the commissioners, sensitive to the rising criticism, wrote back that they planned to roof over the President's House and then put the entire labor force to work finishing up the Capitol building.

Washington wouldn't hear of it. "It was not, nor is it my inten-tion that the work on that house should cease . . . *both* buildings can be completed by the year 1800" was his no-nonsense reply.

As soon as John Adams was inaugurated on March 4, 1797, in Philadelphia as the second President of the United States, former President Washington, accompanied by family and friends, started for Mount Vernon, arriving in the City of Washington on March 14. (Although Washington had modestly called the capital the "Federal City" throughout his term of office, once he was no longer President, he referred to it as the "City of Washington" like every-one else.) In anticipation that the Father of His Country would stop to see *his* house while in the capital, crowds gathered on the grounds along with the Washington Artillery Company captained by James Hoban.

"Yesterday George Washington (God bless him) passed through the city on his way to Mount Vernon," reported the *Washington Gazette.* "As he passed the President's house, a salute of 16 guns was fired by the said company [Hoban's] and followed by repeated huzzas."

Although still only bare stone walls, wood framing for the roof and large empty spaces where windows would one day be set, in many ways the house was like the nation, still unfinished, with much work yet to be done but showing great future promise. And what could be more fitting than to have the new leader of a whole new democratic form of government live and work in a house, not a palace?

2 THE WHITE HOUSE DESTROYED

"THE ENEMY ARE IN FULL MARCH for Washington" was the frightening message that arrived at the White House just before midnight on August 23, 1814.

There was no question as to who the enemy was or what that enemy planned to do. Four thousand British regulars had landed at the mouth of nearby Chesapeake Bay and were now headed toward Washington City with a definite goal in mind. They were determined to burn down all the government buildings in revenge for the American burning of government buildings in the capital of British Upper Canada the year before. And they hoped to capture the President of the United States and his wife, if possible.

Although cannons were mounted at the front gate of the White House and a small force patrolled the grounds, one of the President's household slaves later reported, "Great alarm existed, and some feeble preparations for defense were made." Inside the White House, President James Madison and his wife, Dolley, had tried to maintain a normal routine but at news of the enemy's approach, they gave up all pretence of normalcy and prepared to flee.

Before the War of 1812, two large stone eagles guard the north entrance of the White House.

The War of 1812, which had begun on June 18, 1812, and which was called Mr. Madison's War by his political enemies, was basically being fought with Great Britain over freedom of the seas and America's right to trade where and with whom she pleased. Furthermore, the British had been encouraging Indian attacks on America's western frontier and that had to be stopped, too. Although the war had been dragging on for more than two years, life in the White House had continued much as usual. For the Madisons, that meant a constant round of entertaining, weekly receptions, lawn parties, teas, "Wednesday drawing rooms" and formal dinner parties, where a political and social mix of guests gathered in the "blazing splendor" of the State Rooms.

Earlier White House entertaining had been very different. In November 1800, only four months before his term was up, John Adams, the first President to live in the White House, had moved into what was supposed to be a completed building only to find that the East Room walls were bare brick, a wooden bridge led from the rubble-filled yard to the front door, water had to be carried by hand from nearly half a mile away and the privy was a three-holer in the backyard. Although the major rooms had been wallpapered, almost half of the thirty-six rooms weren't even plastered.

Abigail Adams, who arrived two weeks after her husband, described the drafty "great castle" in a letter to her daughter: "The house is made habitable but there is not a single apartment finished . . . and the great unfinished audience-room [the East Room] I make a drying-room of, to hang up the clothes in." Although Mrs. Adams admitted that "The Presidents House is in a beautifull situation," she also complained, "shiver . . . shiver . . . surrounded by forests, can you believe wood is not to be had, because people cannot be found to cut and cart it." Needless to say, the Adamses didn't entertain often but when they did, they held court much as the Washingtons had in Philadelphia, with Abigail Adams remaining seated and John Adams bowing rather than shaking hands.

After the Adamses' brief four-month stay, in 1801, newly elected President Thomas Jefferson moved into a White House that wasn't much more comfortable. The roof "leaked in such a manner as materially to injure the ceilings and furniture," the wooden bridge to the front door was still in place and the East Room wasn't plastered yet. As late as 1806, a visitor wrote that the grounds were still in such bad condition "that in a dark night instead of finding your way to the house, you may, perchance, fall into a pit, or stumble over a heap of rubbish." As for the house itself, a journalist reported that it was "big enough for two emperors, one pope, and the grand lama," while another visitor noted that Jefferson "inhabits but a corner of the mansion himself and abandons the rest to a state of uncleanly desolation."

Disliking any kind of ceremony or show, Jefferson wrote that he

When the British bombardment of Baltimore's Fort McHenry is over on September 14, 1814, and the American flag still flies, a jubilant Francis Scott Key writes the words to "The Star-Spangled Banner."

"buried . . . levees [receptions], birthdays, royal parades." In their place, he began the White House tradition of holding receptions on New Year's Day and the Fourth of July that were open to the public, with music provided by the splendidly uniformed Marine Band. And Jefferson entertained informally, frequently and well, serving fine French wine and food to mostly male politicians, friends and visitors. A guest commented, "Never before had such dinners been given in the President's House nor such a variety of the finest and most costly wines."

Entertaining in his own democratic style, Jefferson replaced bowing with a handshake, allowed guests to serve themselves from a revolving tray built into the dining room walls and sit where they pleased (much to the horror of foreign diplomats). Great Britain's minister was especially offended by Jefferson's dress which he described as "yarn stockings and slippers down at the heels."

Because Jefferson was a widower, Dolley Madison, as wife of Secretary of State James Madison, often acted as hostess. When her "little Jemmy" became the country's fourth President in 1809, the charming Dolley, already experienced in the ways of the White House, began what was called the "Golden Age" of White House entertaining. (The first known written reference to the title "White House" was during Democratic-Republican Madison's administration in 1811 when a British diplomat wrote, "the crowds round the capital and the *white house* in Washington . . .")

Although Dolley wore elaborate turbans, false curls and dramatic low-cut gowns of silk and satin, a White House guest marveled, "'Tis here the woman who adorns the dress, and not the dress that beautifies the woman." The artist Eastman Johnson wrote, "So polished and elegant are her manners that it is a pleasure to be in her company," while the writer Washington Irving described Dolley as "a fine, portly, buxom dame, who has a smile and a pleasant word for everybody."

But the gracious presidential life-style ended abruptly in August of 1814 with the British march on Washington. In the hot and overcast morning of August 22, a worried President Madison rode out with members of his staff to look over the situation. Dolley, left

James Wood paints
Dolley Madison's portrait
in 1817.

behind in the White House, spent the day rummaging through cupboards and desks for official papers and documents to take with her in case she had to flee. Unfortunately, the one hundred soldiers who had been guarding the grounds had left for Maryland to fight the British, leaving behind only a few men to stand between the White House and the enemy.

The next day, Dolley wrote to her sister that she had received two messages from her husband. ". . . the last [message] is alarming, because he desires I should be ready at a moment's warning to enter my carriage and leave the city . . . I am accordingly ready; I have pressed as many cabinet papers into trunks as will fill one carriage . . . I am determined not to go myself until I see Mr. Madison safe, and he can accompany me—as I hear of much hostility towards him."

The heat persisted into August 24, with thunder rumbling overhead and storm clouds threatening. Although Dolley continued her White House packing, she was frantic for the safety of her husband, who had ridden out to watch the Battle of Bladensburg in nearby Maryland. Dolley expressed her concern in another letter to her sister. "Since sunrise I have been turning my spy-glass in every direction, and watching with unwearied anxiety, hoping to discern the approach of my dear husband and his friends."

In anticipation of their return, she asked the slave Paul Jennings to set the table for thirty-five or forty for the usual three o'clock dinner. In the first memoirs written by a White House insider, but certainly not the last, Paul Jennings, as a free man some years later, recalled, "I set the table myself, and brought up the ale, cider, and wine." At just about three o'clock, a rider pounded up the White House driveway waving his hat and shouting. The President, who had just witnessed an overwhelming American defeat at the Battle of Bladensburg, was sending back orders for everyone to evacuate the White House.

"All then was confusion," Jennings reported.

Dolley, nevertheless, finished her letter. "Will you believe it, my sister? We have had a battle or skirmish near Bladensburg, and I am still here, within sound of the cannons! Mr. Madison comes not; may God protect him! Two messengers, covered with dust, come to bid me fly; but I wait for him. . .

"Our kind friend, Mr. Carroll, has come to hasten my departure, and is in a very bad humor with me because I insist on waiting until the large picture of General Washington is secured, and it requires to be unscrewed from the wall. This process was found too tedious for these perilous moments! I have ordered the frame to be broken, and the canvas taken out: it is done—and the precious portrait placed in the hands of two gentlemen from New York for safe

Because of Dolley Madison's resourcefulness, Gilbert Stuart's portrait of George Washington is the only object that has been in the White House since 1800.

keeping. And now, dear sister, I must leave this house. . . When I shall again write to you, or where I shall be tomorrow, I cannot tell!!"

Paul Jennings's memoirs relate another version of the famous rescue of the Washington portrait from the State Dining Room wall. "It has often been stated in print, that when Mrs. Madison escaped from the White House, she cut out from the frame the large portrait of Washington (now in one of the parlors there), and carried it off. This is totally false. She had no time for doing it. It would have required a ladder to get it down. All she carried off was the silver in her reticule [a net handbag], as the British were thought to be but a few squares off, and were expected every moment. John Susé (a Frenchman, then door-keeper, and still living) and Magraw, the President's gardener, took it down and sent it off on a wagon, with some large silver urns and such other valuables as could be hastily got hold of."

Which version is accurate doesn't really matter. What does matter is that Dolley Madison, knowing that her husband had promised Martha Washington's descendants that the larger-than-lifesize portrait of George Washington would never fall into enemy hands, had made certain that the portrait was carried to safety. The Gilbert Stuart portrait of Washington, which was the first object purchased for the White House, had been bought for $800 by the Secretaries of War, State and Navy in 1800.

By three-thirty on August 24, Dolley Madison had abandoned the White House, taking with her a set of red velvet draperies and two eagle ornaments. She later listed what she'd had to leave behind: "Everything else belonging to the public, our own valuable stores of every description, a part of my clothes, and all the servants' clothes, etc, etc." By now the streets were filled with frightened crowds pulling carts and wagons piled high with their possessions as they fled Washington. Jennings observed, "People were running in every direction."

About four-thirty, a discouraged President Madison and his companions returned to the White House, and although Madison didn't eat the dinner prepared for him, he drank a little wine and rested, leaving for Virginia and safety a few hours later. Soon after, Jennings wrote, "a rabble, taking advantage of the confusion, ran all over the White House, and stole lots of silver and whatever they could lay their hands on."

Almost as soon as the President and his staff had evacuated Washington, the British forces entered the city limits. Sometime around nine P.M., more than one hundred fifty British seamen set fire to the Capitol building and then marched down Pennsylvania Avenue two-by-two to the White House. Breaking into the locked mansion, the sailors spent time looking around just like any other curious tourists. What they stole will never be known, but 125 years later a descendant of one of the British sailors returned President Madison's personal medicine chest to the White House.

Meanwhile, the officers, who sat down at the dining room table, jokingly toasted Madison's health "for being such a good fellow as to leave us such a capital supper." Paul Jennings, who escaped to Virginia that night, described the scene. "When the British did arrive, they ate up the very dinner, and drank the wines, &c., that I had prepared for the President's party."

As soon as the sailors had finished their sightseeing, they systematically smashed the White House windows and "brought together in the salon [Blue Room] all the household goods that were found and prepared to set fire to it." Unfortunately, "household goods" included the handsome new furniture designed for the State Rooms by Benjamin Henry Latrobe, White House architect under both Jefferson and Madison.

Once their task was accomplished, the seamen and their officers hastily left the mansion. Some fifty men had already surrounded the White House, "each carrying a long pole to which was fixed a ball about the circumference of a large plate." The balls, which were rags soaked in oil, were then ignited, the command was given and the men hurled the flaming poles through the broken windows.

An eyewitness described what followed: ". . . the whole building was wrapt in flames and smoke. The spectators stood in awful silence, the city was light and the heavens redden'd with the blaze!" Another bystander commented that the British burned the

On August 24, 1814, the British burn Washington's government buildings, including the White House.

White House "with the ruthless firebrand of the Red Savages of the wood," while the British commander commented to an onlooker, "You may thank Old Madison for this, it is he who got you into this scrape."

A British officer later boasted, "Our sailors were artists at the work." And so they were. The fire was such a roaring blaze, the roof and the entire interior of the White House were totally destroyed. The outer stone walls were saved only because a few hours after the fire was set, the storm that had been threatening all day broke violently, with great flashes of lightning and booming thunder, accompanied by strong winds and a torrential downpour that immediately doused the flames.

Unfortunately, before the rains came, the British had managed to set fire to the War Department Building just west of the White House and the Treasury Building to the east, both of which had been staked out by President Washington eighteen years before. They also burned bridges, an arsenal, a newspaper printing office and every government building in Washington except for the combined Post Office–Patent Office and the Navy Yard, which the Americans had already destroyed to prevent its capture.

The Attorney General, who was across the river in Virginia with the President, described "columns of flame and smoke," with some of the buildings "burning slowly, others with bursts of flames, and sparks mounting high in the dark heavens." At least the British didn't linger long in Washington. Fearful that the American forces might return and worried that the storm had damaged their ships, they departed the capital on August 26.

Of all the buildings that had been left in ruins, the destruction of the White House dealt the most devastating blow to a humiliated nation. The mythic hero, George Washington, had won his country's freedom from the British and now, only some thirty years later, the British had invaded the nation's capital, forced the President and his wife to flee in disgrace and destroyed the very building that George Washington had built and which symbolized the presidency itself.

3 THE WHITE HOUSE IN GOOD TIMES

EVEN THOUGH THE TOUR WOULD TAKE more than three months and cover thirteen states, many of which had only dirt ruts for roads, the newly elected President was determined to make the trip that would take him to the people and bring the people to him. In May of 1817, the President traveled from Washington to Baltimore, on to Philadelphia, New York City, up through New England and into upstate New York, with well-wishers, military bands and marching militia hailing him all along his route.

After sailing across Lake Erie, the President and his party landed at Detroit, continuing from there through the forests of Michigan Territory and Ohio, into Pennsylvania and back, at last, on September 18 to Washington. Endlessly wined, dined and celebrated, the President's goodwill trip was a complete triumph.

A journalist commented, "The President's tour through the East has produced something like a political jubilee."

"ERA OF GOOD FEELINGS," headlined a Boston newspaper.

Because that expression captured the public's imagination, President James Monroe's eight years in office, 1817 to 1825, have

A flatboat on the Ohio River transports a family and its livestock to their new home on the western frontier.

always been known as the Era of Good Feelings. And just as the country flourished and expanded during a time of national pride and unity, so too did the White House.

Certainly after the British burned Washington in August 1814, there were no good feelings anywhere. A Virginia lawyer wrote to a friend, "I went to look at the ruins of the President's House. The rooms which you saw so richly furnished, exhibited nothing but unroofed walls, cracked, defaced and blackened with the fire. I cannot tell you what I felt as I walked among them."

The angry public immediately blamed the Madisons, who had returned to Washington on August 27, the day after the British had left. "The capital and the Union lost by cowardice" was penned on the wall of a burned-out building. Another wall showed a cartoon of Madison running off in such a hurry he was wearing neither hat nor wig. Sensitive to the criticism, the President wrote to his wife the day after the fire when they were apart, "I know not where we are to hide our heads."

Then, with the news of the British defeat by General Andrew Jackson in New Orleans on January 8, 1815, and the message from Europe that a treaty with the British had been signed on Christmas Eve 1814 (two weeks *before* Jackson's victory in New Orleans), Madison-the-villain became Madison-the-hero. His slave Paul Jennings wrote, "When the news of peace arrived, we were crazy with joy . . . such another joyful time was never seen in Washington."

Although neither country had won the war and no territory had exchanged hands, the United States had emerged as an equal partner with Great Britain in world trade and earned worldwide respect as well. Meanwhile, Congress, after a long debate on whether or not to move the capital elsewhere, voted in February 1815 to rebuild the capital in Washington.

A Virginia newspaper reported, "Peace finds us covered with

glory . . . The sun never shone upon a people whose destinies promised to be grander." And with that, a prolonged period of good times began. The economy was soon booming, infant industries sprang up, eastern ports were filled with ships, trade with Europe was thriving and the steamboat was revolutionizing transportation. Farmers and settlers were moving ever westward into the more than eight hundred thousand square miles of Louisiana Territory purchased from France in 1803 under Thomas Jefferson that had more than doubled the size of the United States.

The country's newfound unity witnessed a national bank with a national system of money, a stronger national army and navy and plans for national turnpikes and canals. The Federalist Party, which had opposed the War of 1812 that had ended in an American triumph, was basically dead, leaving the Democratic-Republican Party the only political party in existence.

The American people were anxious for the now-popular Madisons to move out of their rented Washington quarters and return to their proper place in the White House. In 1815, James Hoban, who had become a well-known Washington builder, was hired at a salary of $1,600 a year to reconstruct the burned-out White House exactly as he had built it more than twenty years before.

By 1816, Commissioner Samuel Lane, who had been appointed by President Madison to be in charge of the reconstruction, decided

William Strickland's 1815 engraving dramatically reveals that the burned-out White House is only a smoke-smudged shell.

that as long as even one stone of the original White House remained, it couldn't be said that a new White House was being built. And one stone came frighteningly close to all that was left. Hoban knew, of course, that the interior had been totally destroyed, but when he started work on the walls, he discovered that the heavy rains had cooled the intense fire so quickly, many of the stones had cracked and split. And because the building had stood roofless through two winters, rain, snow and ice had further damaged the walls, with some of the inner brick walls so weakened, they crumbled under the slightest pressure.

Commissioner Lane, who didn't want anyone, especially Congress, to know how serious the damage was, didn't allow Hoban to start tearing down the walls until late April 1816, after Congress had left Washington for the summer. Then it was hurry-hurry-hurry. Hoban, who had wisely directed his stonecutters to cut and stockpile stones the year before, was now able to replace each section of wall as soon as it was torn down.

On the north side of the house, Hoban could save only the center section, which included the front door, the four attached columns on either side of the door and the beautiful stone carvings above the door. The south side suffered only minor damage, with the basement level surviving the best, a tribute to master stonemason Collen Williamson's old groin vaulting of solid stone and brick.

Because the flames had roared up the grand stairway like a flue, the west end of the house was in the worst condition. The entire west wall had to come down, including the huge fan-shaped lunette window on the second floor that had always been one of the building's most appealing features. Although only the center section of the east wall had to go, that involved replacing the east lunette window, too. (Smoke-blackened sections are still visible today on the second floor of the east wall.)

Thanks to a thriving economy, from nine to thirty-two stonecutters were constantly on the job, so that when President Madison finished his second term in March 1817, the stone walls were up, the roof timbers had been raised and the roof temporarily shingled over. Inside the house, the carpentry and cabinetmaking work were well underway, although to save time, Hoban used timber in some of the partitions that separated the rooms instead of brick as he had in the original house.

After President James Monroe was inaugurated on March 4, 1817, the Madisons left their rented house in Washington and retired to Virginia. Although they had never again lived in the White House, the last two years of Madison's administration had begun what would soon be known as the Era of Good Feelings, both for the nation and the White House. A diplomat praised Madison, saying, "Never was a country left in a more flourishing situation than the United States at the end of your administration."

As for Dolley Madison, she returned to the capital in 1836 after her husband's death to again lead Washington society. One of the enduring personalities of the White House, she died in 1849 at the age of eighty-one, "the same good-natured, kind-hearted, considerate, stately person that she had been in the hey-day of her fortunes."

The last President to have been a Revolutionary War veteran and Founding Father, Democratic-Republican James Monroe, as the fifth President of the United States, brought an old-fashioned formality to the White House. One visitor noted, "His dress is plain and in the old style, small clothes, silk hose, knee-buckles, and pumps fastened with buckles." Anxious to move into the White House by the time Congress met again in the fall of 1817, Monroe set an unrealistic deadline of October for finishing the work: ". . . it would be particularly to be regretted if the want of labourers or of materials should retard the progress for a single day," he wrote Commissioner Lane.

While Monroe was on his goodwill tour in the summer of 1817, Congress generously granted Hoban enough funds to hire 190 workers for the White House. With merchants bidding against each other for business and with a healthy competition between European and American goods, prices were kept low, while the steamboat made transportation of materials cheaper and faster.

During that summer of 1817, Hoban installed the windows, constructed the three staircases, placed the four marble columns in

the Entrance Hall, added twelve new fireplaces and painted the exterior walls with a base coat of a linseed oil-and-clay mixture that has since proved to be the most difficult layer of all to remove. But hard as Hoban and his men worked to meet Monroe's deadline, by October 1817, the plaster on the interior walls was still wet, the pine floors weren't painted or carpeted, the woodwork was only primed and none of the twenty-one marble mantels that Monroe had ordered from Italy had arrived.

Finished or not, Monroe understood that the rebuilt White House was a symbol to the American people of their rebuilt nation, and he not only moved into the mansion with his family but he also insisted on holding the traditional public reception on New Year's Day 1818. A newspaper later reported that the White House "was thronged from twelve to three o'clock by an unusually large concourse of gentlemen and ladies . . . It was gratifying to be able once more to salute the President of the United States with the compliments of the season in his appropriate residence."

For the next year and a half, living conditions in the White House were so difficult, it is understandable that Monroe arranged to make a second goodwill tour in 1818, this time through the South. With no carpets and little furniture, the house reeked of plaster, paint, varnish and wallpaper paste and echoed with the racket of hammering, sawing, pounding and workmen's chatter, while fires burned constantly to dry out the wet plaster. Despite the discomfort, Monroe, in a creative burst of energy, increased the White House building projects to include a portico, or porch, at both the north and south entrances. Although the architect Benjamin Henry Latrobe under Jefferson had designed a north and south portico for the White House, neither had ever been built. Now Hoban, whose original plans had also included two porticoes, began work on both.

Hoban, who had already rebuilt the burned-out Treasury and War Department buildings that flanked either side of the White House, was now ordered by Monroe to construct a State Department building north of the Treasury Department and a Navy De-

President James Monroe, known as "the Last of the Cocked Hats," dresses in the 18th-century style as he poses beside a Bellangé chair for the artist John Vanderlyn.

partment building north of the War Department, both of which he finished in 1818.

Monroe next turned his attention to the two wings that had extended out at the basement level from the east and west sides of the White House. Constructed by Latrobe under Jefferson, the original one-story wings had concealed workshops, servants' rooms, privies, stables, a coach house and other service areas. The flat roofs of both wings had served as terraces that could be entered directly from the State Floor for open-air strolling or even entertaining. Now Monroe decided that the two wings, which Hoban had already rebuilt and painted white, should be extended all the way to the Treasury Department building on the east and the War Department building on the west.

It had originally taken Hoban ten years to build the White House. Although the rebuilding took him only three, the cost was about the same, approximately $300,000.

Because Gilbert Stuart's portrait of George Washington was the only object returned to the White House after the fire, Monroe offered to sell the government some of his own belongings to help furnish the completely empty mansion. "I have a small service of excellent plate," he wrote to Commissioner Lane, "dining room, drawing and bedroom furniture, French China and kitchen furniture, all of good quality and in good taste." Although the government agreed to buy Monroe's furnishings for $9,071.22½, he wasn't paid for five years and then only after a great deal of unpleasantness.

Obviously, the White House needed more furniture than what

Monroe could provide personally, so in 1817 Congress granted him $20,000 to buy new furnishings. Monroe, who took great interest in every aspect of the White House, told Congress, "The furniture in its kind and extent is . . . not less deserving attention, than the building for which it is intended."

The President, who had acquired French tastes while serving in Paris as Minister to France, immediately contacted an American firm with offices in France and ordered fifty-one pieces of "strong, massive and durable" furniture from the famous French cabinet-maker Bellangé that included a pier table (a table designed to fit between two openings), chairs, sofas, stools and footstools.

Monroe also ordered French mirrors, screens, curtains, a rug, wallpaper, chandeliers, candelabra, two clocks and numerous other ornamental pieces. At a cost of $1,125, the crowning jewel of Monroe's purchases was a magnificent centerpiece for the dining room table. Called a plateau, the centerpiece of bronze-doré (bronze overlaid with gold) consisted of seven mirrored sections that could be extended to a length of thirteen and a half feet and featured sixteen small figures with detachable vases, candleholders, pedestals and garlands.

The handsome clock ordered from France by James Monroe still keeps perfect time.

With American manufacturers unhappy about all the French purchases for the White House, the official version tried to play down the order. "A vessel has arrived . . . from France with furniture for the house of the President of the United States. Some small matters, we suppose, that could not have been obtained at home," reported a Baltimore newspaper. Considering that ninety-three crates arrived from France at a cost of $19,716, "small matters" seemed somewhat of an understatement.

On the other hand, many people approved wholeheartedly. A visitor to the White House commented, "The plates were handsome china, the forks silver, and so heavy that I could hardly lift them to my mouth, dessert knives silver, and spoons very heavy." A senator remarked that the "splendidly furnished" Oval Room was "designed to impress upon foreign ministers a respect for the Government, which may have a valuable influence upon our foreign relations."

When Congress appropriated another $30,000 for furnishings in 1818, an enthusiastic Monroe had no trouble spending it, this time mostly on American-made products, including a new $150 frame for George Washington's portrait and marble busts of Columbus, Americus Vespucius and George Washington for which he paid $300 to the son of George Washington's secretary. At the same time, Monroe was careful to reassure Congress that his purchases would "last, with care, more than twenty and some of them perhaps fifty years." Those purchases remain today at the heart of the White House treasures, particularly the bronze-doré plateau which has seen continuous use at formal White House dinners ever since 1817.

And then in 1819, the Bank of the United States failed, there was an economic depression and the White House, like everything else, felt the pinch. Construction of the wings stopped only halfway to the Treasury and War Department buildings, just about where they had ended under Jefferson. The newly named East Room was neither completed nor furnished. Although work on both porticoes came to a halt with only the floors and makeshift roofs finished, in 1824 Hoban was granted enough funds to complete the South Portico. Six Ionic columns soared up forty feet from the half-circle porch outside the oval Blue Room to a half-circle roof on the third floor.

Surprisingly enough, because no one seemed to blame Monroe for the economic depression or for other national problems that were surfacing, particularly the explosive issue of slavery, which was temporarily defused by the Missouri Compromise of 1820, the expression the Era of Good Feelings continued to describe Monroe's presidency. Probably best remembered for the Monroe Doctrine, which warned European powers to keep "hands-off" the Americas, Monroe ended his administration much as it had begun, with a flourish of pageantry.

In 1824 and 1825, as "the nation's guest" and the living symbol of French support during the American Revolution, the Marquis de Lafayette made a triumphant tour of all twenty-four states in the most festive celebration the country had ever staged. But in

1825, with Lafayette's return to France and the end of Monroe's second term, America was suddenly bidding farewell to all ties to the American Revolution as well as a certain 18th-century idealism and courtliness.

Although the Era of Good Feelings was over, while it had lasted, national pride, a booming economy, westward expansion and a generous Congress had served both the country and the White House well. Rebuilt exactly as it had been designed originally, with the South Portico finished and Monroe's unique works of art gracing the State Rooms, the reconstructed White House reflected one of the nation's happiest and most prosperous periods.

4 THE WHITE HOUSE AND THE COMMON PEOPLE

"I HAVE NEVER SEEN SUCH A CROWD BEFORE" was Senator Daniel Webster's reaction to the thousands of people who had flocked to Washington for the inauguration of "the People's President" on March 4, 1829. Once the swearing-in ceremony at the Capitol was over, the people swarmed down Pennsylvania Avenue to meet the new President at the White House. With the people hurling themselves on the food and drink, crystal and china were smashed, women fainted and fights broke out that bloodied noses and furniture, while men with "boots heavy with mud" stood on "satin-covered chairs" to see better.

The President, who was trying to greet people in the Blue Room, was soon backed up against the wall and *literally* nearly pressed to death and almost suffocated." Only aides locking arms and forming "a kind of barrier of their own bodies" got him safely out a rear window. With servants placing washtubs of punch on the south lawn to lure the crowds outside, the President's absence was hardly noticed.

"A rabble, a mob, of boys, negros, women, children, scrambling,

Artist Robert Cruikshank titles his painting of the President's 1829 inaugural reception "The President's Levee—or all Creation going to the White House."

51

fighting, romping. What a pity what a pity!" a member of Washington society wrote. "But it was the People's day, and the People's President and the People would rule."

A frontier Kentucky newspaper viewed the reception of the newly inaugurated Andrew Jackson differently. "It was a proud day for the people. General Jackson is *their own* president . . . the Hero of a popular triumph."

Many years later a White House butler wrote, "The transformation in the household from one Administration to another is as sudden as death." And that was certainly true when the seventh President of the United States, Democrat Andrew Jackson, arrived at the White House. During the administrations of four aristocratic Virginians (Washington, Jefferson, Madison and Monroe) and two Harvard graduates (John Adams and his son John Quincy Adams), farmers, craftsmen, tradespeople and merchants had prospered into a new and growing middle class.

Because most states had eliminated property ownership as a voting requirement by 1828, more than three times the number of votes had been cast in the 1828 election than had been cast in 1824 (only white adult males were allowed to vote). And the majority of those votes had been for frontiersman Andrew Jackson, who, with his "abiding confidence in the virtue and intelligence of the American people," believed that government should no longer be an "engine for the support of the few at the expense of the many."

Jackson was not only the first to reach the presidency from the open frontier, but he was also the first to be elected by popular vote. (The first five Presidents had been elected by the Electoral College with no popular vote recorded, while the 1824 election had been decided in the House of Representatives because there had been no clear majority.) Symbolizing the American dream that anyone could become President, Jackson, by his determination, drive and physical strength, had risen from poverty in the wilderness to become a military hero in 1814 at the Battle of New Orleans. With his soldiers bragging that their general was as "tough as hickory," Jackson had acquired the lifelong nickname of "Old Hickory."

When Thomas Jefferson had been elected President twenty-eight years earlier, he had written, ". . . our liberty can never be safe but in the hands of the people themselves." And Jefferson, by introducing a certain informality to the presidency, as well as by opening the mansion to the public, had run a more democratic White House than either Washington or Adams before him.

Four administrations later, Andrew Jackson carried democracy in the White House even further. Although he was both a slaveholder and an Indian fighter, he not only believed that the people were "capable of self-government" but he also considered it was his duty to protect "the liberties and rights of the people." That Jackson was hot-tempered, egotistical and stubborn was no secret, with a political friend admitting, "When Jackson begins to talk about hanging, they can begin to look for the ropes."

On the other hand, a niece-by-marriage made it clear that although Jackson was known as a man of "iron will and fierce, ungovernable temper . . . he was the gentlest, tenderest, most patient of men at his own fireside." Jackson so mourned his beloved wife Rachel, who died only weeks after his election, that he always carried her picture next to his heart. (Rachel had once said, "I had rather be a doorkeeper in the house of God than to live in that palace in Washington.") Devastated by Rachel's death, Jackson, whose health had never been good, was a grief-stricken and sickly sixty-one years old when he entered the White House in 1829. At the time, Vice President Martin Van Buren remarked about the widowed Jackson's relationship with the people, "They were his blood relations—the only blood relations he had."

Despite his physical frailty, Jackson had definite ideas about what he wanted to do, both as President and in the White House. Demanding funds from Congress, Jackson's first priority was to finish the North Portico at the front entrance that James Hoban had started in 1818. Within a month of Jackson's inauguration, Hoban, now almost seventy, took on his last assignment in the

BORN TO COMMAND.

OF VETO MEMORY.

HAD I BEEN CONSULTED.

KING ANDREW THE FIRST.

A political cartoon portrays Andrew Jackson as "King Andrew the First" trampling on the Constitution, the Supreme Court and the National Bank.

historic building that he had begun thirty-seven years earlier. (He died two years later.)

When it was finished in September 1829, the rectangular portico, with its 50-foot-high columns, measured 40 feet by 59 feet and served as a porch for the main entrance and a porte cochère (a covered shelter under which vehicles may be driven). The bold and massive North Portico, which would be the last exterior change at the White House for seventy-three years, gave dignity and character to the front of the mansion, just as the curving South Portico added grace to the back.

Almost immediately, Jackson began decorating the dreary East Room that had been completed in 1818 but had never been furnished. Perhaps in reaction to all of Monroe's French purchases, Congress had passed a law in 1826 stating that furniture "purchased for use in the President's House shall be as far as possible of American or domestic manufacture." With that in mind, for some $9,000, Jackson had the East Room furnished from that new American one-stop shopping convenience, the furniture warehouse. Chairs, sofas, tables, three chandeliers that lit the room with "remarkable brilliancy," four large mirrors, almost five hundred square yards of carpeting and twenty spittoons filled the huge room. Jackson was also eager to repair Monroe's French chairs so that people wouldn't be kept "standing upon their legs as they do before kings and emperors."

In the Green Room, which had been named in the 1820s, Jackson chose a shade of green for the walls that made the ladies unhappy "from the sallow look it imparts." During Jackson's administration, the formal dining room became officially known as the State Dining Room. The Blue Room acquired its name in 1837 while the Red Room was called the Washington Parlor until the 1840s.

As for entertaining, Jackson considered the White House the "People's House" and himself "their steward," making it clear that anyone off the street was welcome with no invitations needed to his three public receptions on New Year's Day, the Fourth of July and the Anniversary of the Battle of New Orleans. And he treated all his guests with the same respect, including "rag-a-muffins," "Indians in war-dress" and "fellows with dirty faces and dirty manners." One visitor described the guests as including everyone "from the vice President to an intoxicated canal labourer in a dirty red cloak," which was exactly how Andrew Jackson wanted it.

Right from the beginning, Jackson made himself available at all hours to anyone who walked into the White House to meet him, air a complaint or simply shake his hand. Nevertheless, Jackson, like the democratic Jefferson, also appreciated fine wines and a handsomely set table, purchasing in 1833 a magnificent French silver service from the estate of a Russian diplomat, as well as handsome French china and crystal.

During Jackson's administration, the White House grounds underwent changes, too. Abigail Adams had written in 1800, "The Country round is romantic but a wild wilderness at present." The property still didn't look like much when Jefferson arrived in 1801, although an acquaintance commented that Jefferson "was very anxious to improve the ground around the President's House." Under Jefferson's direction, architect Benjamin Henry Latrobe had surrounded the White House property with a stone wall that stood for almost seventy-five years. Jefferson had also separated what he called the President's Park into its traditional division. The south grounds were for the President's private use, while the north front yard was for the public. Under Jefferson's supervision, rolling hummocks, called the Jefferson Mounds, had been built on the south lawn, which still protect those walking near the White House from public view.

Of all the Presidents before or since, John Quincy Adams took the greatest interest in the gardens and grounds. By planting almost every kind of known tree and shrub, including an elm tree on the south lawn that is the oldest presidential tree at the White House today, Adams virtually created a museum of American plants. A contemporary wrote, "John Quincy Adams loved gardening, and gratified his taste in a White House garden every spring and summer morning, after he had taken his swim in the Potomac . . ." Perhaps it was his gardening and his daily swim in

Andrew Jackson poses in a Bellangé chair for a portrait by Ralph E. W. Earl, a relative by marriage who is a frequent visitor at the White House.

the Potomac River that helped Adams survive what he called the "four most miserable years of my life."

During his presidency Jackson planted two magnolia trees by the South Portico in memory of his wife that have grown as tall as the White House itself and are known as the Jackson Magnolias. Jackson, who directed the permanent location of the driveway leading to the north entrance, also directed the building of extensive fences, shelters, benches, a hothouse, footpaths, gardens and new stables. The old stables had been so close to the State Dining Room, unmistakable odors used to waft through the open windows much to the distress of the dinner guests inside. In 1835, an elaborate system of reservoirs and iron pipes pumped spring water directly into the White House, making Jackson the first President to enjoy the luxury of running water.

Not surprisingly, Jackson ended his presidency much as he had begun it, with the White House welcoming "the people." In 1835 a 1,400-pound cheddar cheese that was four feet in diameter and two feet thick had been sent as a gift to Jackson who had it placed in the Entrance Hall. In celebration of George Washington's birthday in 1837, Jackson invited the public-at-large into the White House to sample the cheese. And sample they did. As the local newspaper reported, "All you heard was cheese; all you smelled was cheese." Within two hours it was gone, leaving cheese mashed into the carpet, grease stains on the floor and an odor that lasted for weeks.

But Jackson left more than grease stains in the White House to

The 1,400-pound cheese that Andrew Jackson receives as a gift doesn't last long once he invites the public into the White House to sample it.

remember him by. When he retired to Tennessee in 1837 after eight stormy years in the White House, he was so frail he was often unable to stand up. And yet his indomitable spirit had made him such a strong President, he was perhaps second only to George Washington in his historic influence on the presidency.

Jackson's famous toast, *"Our* Federal *Union*—It must be preserved," backed up by a threat of military action against South Carolina rather than permit that state to defy federal tariff laws, remains one of his most important achievements. Drawing his support, not from any one region but from the whole nation, Jackson, who used his veto power more than all previous Presidents combined, allowed the common people, whom he called "the bone and sinew of the country," to take part in their government for the first time.

When Jackson died in 1845, a laborer wrote about the People's President, "the Hon Major General andrew Jackson is gone and his voice are heared no more on earth. But his name still lives in the heart of the American people."

It did indeed. Although a second political party, the Whig Party, had developed in opposition to Jackson's policies in the 1830s, the Democrats held a tight grip on the presidency until the end of James Buchanan's administration in 1861, even through the unpopular 1846-to-1848 Mexican War under President James Polk. Only two Whig Party candidates, William Henry Harrison and Zachary Taylor, both Indian fighters and military heroes who reminded the people of Old Hickory, were elected President during that period. The Whig Party broke up in the 1850s over the issue of slavery.

In 1840 Democratic President Martin Van Buren was accused by Congressman Charles Ogle of "regal splendor" in the White House and of using "the People's cash" to buy "knives, forks, and spoons of gold, that he may dine in the style of the monarchs of Europe" while decent Americans were eating "hog and hominy" and "fried meat and gravy." Actually, Van Buren had spent less than half of what that backwoodsman Andrew Jackson had spent on the White

House, but Ogle's famous "Golden Spoon" speech convinced "the people" to defeat Van Buren in his bid for re-election.

Because politicians are fast learners, the eight Presidents who followed Jackson, all of whom served for only one term and who were, with the exception of James Polk, mostly forgettable, directed their campaigns to those voters who were carving homes out of the frontier and considered themselves the equal of any easterner. By claiming the same humble beginnings as Jackson, whether or not it was true, candidates ran for office with the home-spun nicknames of "Old Kinderhook" (Van Buren), "Old Tip" and "Farmer From North Bend" (William Henry Harrison), "Old Rough and Ready" (Zachary Taylor), with two candidates (James Polk and Franklin Pierce) calling themselves "Young Hickory." And their slogans appealed to the fighting frontier, too: "Log Cabin and Hard Cider", "Tippecanoe and Tyler Too!", "All of Oregon, All of Texas!", "54° 40' or Fight!"

William Henry Harrison (Tippecanoe), the son of a wealthy Virginia planter, runs for President in the hotly contested 1840 election with the frontier slogan of "Log Cabin and Hard Cider" (which he dislikes).

Although in one sense the Age of Jackson ended in the 1850s, in another sense it has never ended. With the election of Andrew Jackson in 1828, for the first time the Constitution's "We the People of the United States" had claimed the presidency as their own. "The People" had thrown open the doors of the White House and they would never be closed again.

5 THE WHITE HOUSE IN MOURNING

BY FIVE O'CLOCK ON THE MORNING of April 18, 1865, the silent crowds that had been gathering at the White House for hours were lined up six or seven deep for a mile. Right at nine-thirty, the White House driveway gates swung open and the people began to file toward the black-draped North Portico, through the front door and into the Entrance Hall.

Directed by military guards, they passed into the Green Room and from there into the black-draped East Room. The crystal chandeliers were wrapped in black, as were the frames of the eight mirrors, with white cloth covering the mirrors themselves. In the center of the room a coffin rested on a black-draped catafalque, a sixteen-foot-long platform with such a high canopy, the middle chandelier had been removed and its gas line capped.

An occasional sob broke the silence as the people made their way to the foot of the catafalque, split into two lines, mounted a step and walked slowly beside the open coffin. The mourners, with only a moment to gaze down at the still face of their martyred President

The President's funeral in the East Room on April 19, 1865, is attended by every dignitary in the nation, and although the artist includes a heavily veiled First Lady, she remains in her bedroom throughout the ceremony.

before the crush of people moved them on, had no time to read the engraving on the coffin's silver shield:

Abraham Lincoln
Sixteenth President of the United States
Born Feb. 12, 1809
Died April 15, 1865

Never had the country suffered through such a prolonged period of mourning as it had experienced during the Civil War. As brother fought brother, almost every American home, including the home of the President, had lost loved ones. And then, five days after the war was essentially over, when there was at last hope that there could be "a lasting peace" under a compassionate President who had pledged "to bind up the nation's wounds," that President was assassinated.

The grief that filled the White House was described by Mrs. Lincoln's seamstress, Elizabeth Keckley. "Every room in the White House was darkened and every one spoke in subdued tones, and moved about with muffled tread." As for the city of Washington, a newspaper reporter wrote that when word went out that the President had been shot, the streets "were suddenly crowded with people—men, women, and children thronging the pavements and darkening the thoroughfares. It seemed as if everybody was in tears. Pale faces, streaming eyes . . ." Washington's sorrow was echoed across the country. "Ah! never was man so widely mourned before. The whole world bowed their heads in grief when Abraham Lincoln died."

Twenty-four years earlier, President William Henry Harrison had died a month after his inauguration on April 4, 1841, an event that had stunned and bewildered the country. No President had ever died in office before. What now? Should Vice President John Tyler be Acting President until the next election or should he be President in fact? The Constitution stated, "In case of the Removal

During the Civil War, many soldiers are buried in makeshift army graveyards.

of the President from Office, or of his Death, Resignation, or Inability to discharge the Powers and Duties of the said Office, the same shall devolve on the Vice President . . ." Did that mean "same powers and duties" or "same office"? Because James Madison, the last surviving framer of the Constitution, had died five years earlier, there was no one left to explain what the wording meant.

But Tyler didn't hesitate. Despite being called "His Accidency" by his political opponents, Tyler, who insisted that he was President in his own right, took the presidential oath of office on April 6, 1841, two days after President Harrison's death. Because of that long-ago decision, nine Vice Presidents, including Tyler, have taken the presidential oath of office on the death or resignation of a President: Millard Fillmore after Zachary Taylor's death in 1850, Andrew Johnson after Abraham Lincoln's assassination in 1865, Chester A. Arthur after James Garfield's assassination in 1881, Theodore Roosevelt after William McKinley's assassination in 1901, Calvin Coolidge after Warren Harding's death in 1923, Harry S. Truman after Franklin D. Roosevelt's death in 1945, Lyndon B. Johnson after John F. Kennedy's assassination in 1963.

In 1967 the Twenty-fifth Amendment to the Constitution at last clearly stated that "the Vice President shall become President" in case of the President's death or resignation, an event that occurred only seven years later when President Richard Nixon resigned and Vice President Gerald Ford was sworn in as President.

President Harrison's 1841 funeral set the pattern for all the presidential funerals that followed, with black banners draped on the White House exterior and black covering the White House mirrors, chandeliers and paintings. Harrison's open coffin was placed in the Entrance Hall so that the public could pay its respects, with hundreds of invited guests attending the formal funeral service held later in the East Room. A newspaper reported, "After the services the coffin was carried to a large funeral car drawn by six white horses, each having at its head a black groom dressed in white, with white turban and sash." Thousands of people lined Washington's streets as the procession of dignitaries followed Harrison's coffin to the Congressional Burying Ground.

Some twenty years later, Abraham Lincoln, the first Republican President of the United States, had a foreboding of his own death. Soon after his 1863 Emancipation Proclamation freed all the slaves in the Confederate states, Lincoln told the writer Harriet Beecher Stowe, "Whichever way it [the war] ends, I have the impression I shan't last long after it's over."

Only two weeks before his death, Lincoln had confided to his wife and a friend that he had dreamed that he was awakened by the sound of "pitiful sobbing" from somewhere in the White House. Going from room to room, he had followed the sobbing to the East Room, where he had come upon a catafalque surrounded by mourners and military guards. In response to Lincoln's inquiry as to who was dead in the White House, a soldier had replied, "The President, he was killed by an assassin!" Lincoln reported that he had slept no more that night.

It was understandable that Lincoln, who received untold numbers of death threats, dreamed about death. Before his first inauguration in 1861, he had been smuggled into Washington during the night to avoid changing trains in Baltimore where a plot to murder him had been uncovered. And in the early years of the Civil War, when there was a chance that Washington and the White House might be invaded by Confederate troops, Union soldiers had camped in the East Room and on the South Lawn. "The White House has turned into a barrack," wrote Lincoln's secretary.

By opening the White House to virtually anyone who wanted to walk in, President Andrew Jackson and the Presidents who had followed him had exposed themselves to the possibility of violence. President Tyler had called for a captain and three men to act as the first permanent White House security guards. Although the unit was the beginning of Washington's Metropolitan Police force, they were known as White House doormen to avoid appearing too military. In the 1850s, a federal employee served as a full-time bodyguard to President Franklin Pierce, who could hardly be blamed for his caution. Pierce had, after all, witnessed an assassination attempt in 1835 at the Capitol when a mentally disturbed young man had shot at President Andrew Jackson at close range, failing only because both of his pistols misfired.

A Metropolitan Police bodyguard always accompanied President Lincoln, his wife, Mary, and their three sons, Robert, Willie and Tad, anytime they left the White House, with one guard commenting, "We were ordered to report in citizens' clothes, to conceal our

When an attempt on his life fails, President Andrew Jackson (center) takes after the would-be assassin with his walking stick, January 1835.

John Wilkes Booth fires a
fatal shot at Abraham
Lincoln on April 14, 1865,
also inflicting a deep
dagger wound on Major
Henry Rathbone, who
leaps to the President's
defense.

revolvers, and to be sure to have them all clean and in good order."
Despite the protection, Lincoln, like Presidents before and since,
admitted to a reporter, "I long ago made up my mind that if anyone
wants to kill me he will do it." He was right. Lincoln's bodyguard
had left his post at Ford's Theater on April 14, 1865, when John
Wilkes Booth entered the President's box, pointed a pistol at the
back of Lincoln's head and fired. Lincoln, who never regained con-
sciousness, died the following morning.

The Commander in Chief had fallen in battle just as surely as the
more than five hundred thousand young Americans who had died
during the Civil War, in combat, in prison camps, from wounds or
from disease, the highest number of dead in any American war.
Abraham Lincoln, who had grieved for North and South losses
alike, once said, "When I think of the sacrifice yet to be offered and
the hearts and homes yet to be made desolate before this dreadful
war is over, my heart is like lead within me."

Like almost every other home, the White House had experienced
death, too. Elmer Ellsworth, a member of the White House staff
who was loved by the Lincolns as a son, was one of the first officers
killed in the war, while Mary Lincoln lost three close relatives
fighting for the South. And bright, gentle, eleven-year-old Willie
Lincoln died in the White House in 1862 of what was described as
"bilious fever." At his death, a shattered Lincoln "buried his head
in his hands, and his tall frame was convulsed with emotion,"
recalled Elizabeth Keckley. "It is hard, hard to have him die!" the
President had cried.

Yet through his pain, Lincoln realized that the White House was
a symbol of unity and stability and insisted on keeping the mansion
open to the public, maintaining it in good condition and entertaining often. Even in wartime, his bodyguard reported that "anyone
who wished to talk to Lincoln could walk up to his office, and after
speaking with the doorkeeper go in and meet him."

Congress, also aware of the symbolic importance of the White
House, allotted the Lincolns the usual $20,000 given to all incom-
ing Presidents for furnishings and repairs. But Mary Lincoln, who
was a compulsive shopper, quickly overspent her budget. In addi-

tion to her redecoration of the East Room in 1861, she bought a set of furniture for the Prince of Wales Room (the Prince of Wales had slept there in 1860) that included a massive bed draped with purple-and-gold satin curtains, matching draperies, a marble-topped table and six chairs.

The famous furniture that Mary Lincoln purchases in 1861 is photographed in 1898 looking much as it does today.

The usually patient Lincoln was furious. "It would stink in the nostrils of the American people to have it said that the President of the United States had approved a bill over-running an appropriation of $20,000 for *flub-dubs* for this damned old house, when the soldiers cannot have blankets," he fumed. There was no way that either of the Lincolns could know that the ornate rosewood furniture has long had a place of honor in the Lincoln Bedroom and Sitting Room.

But furniture wasn't uppermost in anyone's mind after Willie's death. Although Lincoln was so heartsick that he visited his son's grave often, he did his best to comfort his increasingly unstable wife. During a carriage ride they took on the afternoon before he was shot, Lincoln had said to her, "We must both be more cheerful in the future; between the war and the loss of our darling Willie, we have been very miserable." But as Lincoln lay dying through that long April night, Mary had surrendered to hysteria, and in the days to come, had remained so hysterical, she was unable to make any decisions concerning the funeral except for ordering that her husband be buried in Springfield, Illinois, where the Lincolns had made their home for many years.

As a result, planning the funeral was left up to Major William French, Commissioner of Public Buildings, who immediately researched the presidential funerals of Harrison and Taylor to follow as a guide. But Harrison and Taylor had died of natural causes and Lincoln had been shot! Assassinated in the presence of his wife! Lincoln's funeral would not only have to restore dignity to the office of the presidency and to the White House, but it would also have to allow a devastated nation to participate in the mourning.

While Washington was being flooded with one hundred thousand citizens arriving to pay last respects to their President (six thousand spent the night in parks, vacant lots and public buildings), elaborate preparations were being made at the White House. After an autopsy was performed upstairs in the Prince of Wales Room, the President's body was placed on the newly built catafalque in a silver-handled walnut coffin for the public viewing in the East Room. A newspaper reported, "The throngs pressing to see the body of the President is beyond all precedent. It required waiting for not less than six hours to get in."

After the doors were closed to the public at five-thirty P.M., special groups paid their respects for the next two hours, with carpenters arriving that evening to construct stands in the East Room that would give all six hundred invited guests a view of the open coffin during the funeral service. To Mary Lincoln, upstairs in bed, every hammer blow sounded like the pistol shot that had taken her husband's life and she begged them to stop. But any influence Mrs. Lincoln might have once had was gone and the hammering continued through the night.

With the exception of Mrs. Lincoln, young Tad and Secretary of State Seward, who had been wounded by one of the conspirators, every person of importance in the nation, including newly sworn-in President Andrew Johnson, attended the funeral on April 19. A reporter described the scene. "The high coffin was covered with black, trimmed with pure silver lace . . . A cross of lilies stood at the head, and an anchor of roses at the foot. The lid of the coffin was thrown back to show the face and bosom of the deceased."

At the conclusion of the simple two-hour service in which there was neither music nor singing, the coffin was placed on a funeral car that was waiting at the north entrance. The hearse, which was drawn by six white horses and followed by a groom leading Lincoln's riderless gray gelding with his master's boots reversed in the stirrups, was accompanied by a military escort carrying their firearms reversed. Making their slow way down the driveway to the gate, the marchers turned right on Pennsylvania Avenue and headed for the Capitol.

On that beautiful April day, one hundred thousand spectators watched the three-mile-long procession with its more than thirty thousand marchers that took more than two hours to pass any given point. Family members (all but Mary Lincoln, who remained in her bedroom), officials, the military, thirty bands, five thousand government workers, fire hose companies, fraternal lodges, church bodies, black organizations, schoolchildren, teachers, singing societies, Indians, wounded soldiers and countless others marched to the music of the Marine Band, the tattoo of muffled drums, big siege guns booming and every bell in the city tolling. Perhaps it was fitting that black regiments brought up both the front and rear of a procession that was paying honor to the man who had freed the slaves two years before. "The Moses of my people has fallen in the hour of his triumph," cried a black mourner.

After lying in state in the Capitol Rotunda, where three thousand citizens an hour filed by, both Lincoln's flag-draped coffin and

Drawn by six white horses, Lincoln's funeral car is eleven feet high to allow the public to view the President's coffin on its way from the White House to the Capitol Rotunda.

Willie Lincoln's small coffin, which had been removed from its above-ground vault, were placed on a special railroad car for the trip back to Springfield, Illinois, for burial. The long journey, which was to begin on April 21, would retrace the route that Lincoln had taken on his way from Springfield to Washington for his first inauguration in 1861, with the same stops along the way: Baltimore, Harrisburg, Philadelphia, New York, Albany, Buffalo, Cleveland, Columbus, Indianapolis, Chicago and Springfield.

Although the train only traveled ten to twenty miles an hour throughout the twelve-day trip, so many people wanted to view the car in which the coffin rested, at times the train could hardly move. Elaborate arches were constructed for the train to pass under, while "a pillar of fire by night" was created by the setting of huge bonfires along the railroad tracks, bystanders holding aloft torches and lanterns and houses bordering the train's route lit from within by candles and lamps. Each of the eleven cities where the train was to stop had built an elaborate hearse that would carry the coffin in a carefully planned procession to an appropriate resting place where the President's coffin would be opened so that the people of the city could pay their respects.

During that sad journey, Mrs. Lincoln remained secluded in her bedroom while chaos reigned in the State Rooms below. Unwilling to evict the widow, President Andrew Johnson had set up offices in the Treasury Building next door, so that the White House was virtually empty of all government business. Nevertheless, the doors remained open and tourists flooded in during the public hours ransacking and looting souvenirs from the East Room, which for ten days remained set up with its funeral trappings. Silver, china and other valuables were stolen, draperies ripped, furniture gashed. Commissioner French commented that by May there were no lamps, vases or small objects left in the East Room. "All curtains badly cut—rest of furniture pretty badly used," he noted. By the time the always-unpopular Mrs. Lincoln finally left the White House on May 22, rumors were already circulating that she had taken numerous cartons of White House valuables with her.

In happier White House days, Abraham Lincoln looks through a photograph album with his youngest son, Tad.

But at that moment in time, the nation wasn't focused on the White House, it was focused on the slow-moving presidential train as it traveled from city to city. In Philadelphia, half a million people, which was the current population of Philadelphia, gathered to watch the procession, with one hundred and twenty thousand mourners passing through Independence Hall, where Lincoln's body lay in state, a particularly moving experience. In 1861 Lincoln had declared in a speech at Independence Hall, "Sooner than surrender these principles, I would be assassinated first." In New York the lines to view Lincoln's body stretched for a mile twenty abreast, with all the ships in the harbor draped in black.

Even though the train traveled through less and less populated areas as it headed west, thousands of mourners continued to line the railroad tracks, many of them kneeling in prayer and singing hymns. A military escort riding on the train noted, "The intensity of feeling seemed, if possible, to grow deeper as the President's remains went further westward where the people more especially claimed him as their own."

At last the train reached Springfield, where both Abraham Lincoln and Willie were buried in an emotional ceremony on May 4, 1865. A reporter who made the almost two-thousand-mile journey aboard the train wrote, "The funeral was continuous from Washington to Oak Ridge Cemetery."

With a national population of approximately thirty-five million, a million people had viewed Lincoln's body, with seven million more participating in some way in a national outpouring of grief that had begun in the White House and traveled by slow-moving train across the country. Citizens everywhere had wept tears of grief, not only for their slain President, but also for all the young lives that had been snuffed out by war. And perhaps without realizing it, the nation was mourning too, for the loss of a rural innocence and simplicity that it would never know again.

Escorted by a military guard and witnessed by a hundred thousand mourners, Lincoln's funeral procession makes its way through the streets of New York City.

6 THE WHITE HOUSE AS A STAGE

ALTHOUGH THE WHITE HOUSE RECEPTION for diplomats was the social event of any Washington season, this year's reception on January 8, 1903, promised to outdo all others. With the White House newly restored and with a President who could always be counted on for a colorful performance, the guests anticipated an entertaining evening.

They weren't disappointed. After entering the White House through the new East Wing entrance, the guests were directed up the marble stairs to the State Floor by handsome young military aides in brilliant uniforms. Already seated in the Entrance Hall, the forty-piece Marine Band awaited its signal to introduce the President.

On the stroke of eight, trumpets blared and drums rolled as the iron gates of the new grand stairway swung back and the presidential party started down the stairs. First came two military aides in gold braid and polished leather, followed by special guests, the men in white tie and formal black and the women wearing elegant gowns and ropes of pearls. And then, as the Marine Band swung

For many years a temporary bridge from the East Room to the north driveway is used by departing guests at large receptions.

into "Hail to the Chief," the anthem that had announced presidential entrances since the 1840s, the President and his wife appeared dramatically at the top of the stairs and began their descent. It was hard to tell who enjoyed the moment more, the enthralled guests or the twenty-sixth President of the United States, Theodore Roosevelt.

On the death of President William McKinley on September 14, 1901, Vice President Theodore Roosevelt had become President, seemingly the right man at the right time. Although the eight Presidents since Lincoln's time had been basically caretaker-Presidents, with only Ulysses S. Grant and Grover Cleveland serving more than one term, the country itself had gone through enormous changes as it shifted from an agricultural to an industrial economy. As optimistic, brash and full of confidence as Roosevelt himself, the nation, which was now settled from coast to coast, witnessed the growth of cities, railroad systems, factories and steel mills, as well as the development of electrical power, the telephone and the automobile.

After winning the Spanish-American War in 1898, America, as a new world power, had annexed Hawaii and acquired the Philippines, Guam and Puerto Rico. It was a period when America was beginning to hold center stage as a new world power, and with the White House for a setting, the enthusiastic leading man couldn't wait to play out his role. "We stand at the threshold of a new century," Roosevelt had said in 1900. "Our nation, glorious in youth and strength, looks into the future with fearless and eager eyes, and rejoices as a strong man to run a race."

But all was not smooth sailing the following year when the Roosevelts arrived at the White House, where security had tightened after the assassination of McKinley. The Treasury Department's Secret Service, which had previously shared protection of the President with the Metropolitan Police and the White House ushers, had now taken over full responsibility. "The secret service are a very small but very necessary thorn in the flesh," Roosevelt wrote to a friend.

And the White House itself wasn't the perfect setting the Roosevelts had anticipated. For years politicians, tradesmen, officials, tourists and favor-seekers waiting to see the President in his second-floor offices had noisily gathered in the Entrance Hall. And with hundreds of thousands of sightseers a year trooping through the State Rooms, as well as thousands of guests attending official functions, the shabby White House was no longer even safe. Because the floors were settling so dangerously, the State Dining Room and the East Room had to be propped up every time there was a party, with a temporary wooden bridge constructed as an exit from the East Room out to the north driveway to handle the crowds at large receptions.

On the Family Floor, the large Roosevelt clan was crowded into only eight rooms, with the other rooms used for presidential offices.

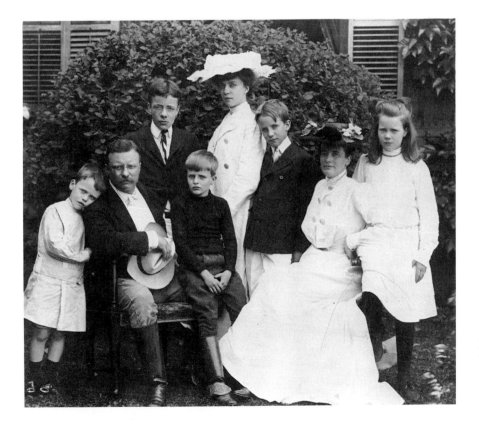

Theodore Roosevelt relaxes with his wife and six children on the lawn of his Oyster Bay, Long Island, home.

There were few bathrooms and no closets, all the flooring needed to be replaced, the sanitary conditions were unhealthy, old wiring had dangerously charred wooden beams, while a lack of exits in the attic made the servants' rooms a firetrap.

Roosevelt certainly wasn't the first President to face difficult living conditions. Presidents Chester Arthur, Benjamin Harrison, Grover Cleveland and William McKinley had all suggested additions to the White House or even an entirely new mansion. But Roosevelt insisted that the White House of George Washington and Abraham Lincoln was of symbolic importance to the nation. "Mrs. Roosevelt and I are firmly of the opinion that the President should live nowhere else than in the historic White House," he declared. Congress agreed, appropriating $475,445 in June 1902 for repairs and renovations.

Charles McKim, a famous New York architect who had been called in earlier to help with White House decorating, was now assigned the job of reconstruction. Although he had little interest in the architectural history of the White House, he carefully used the word "restoration" as he designed a complete transformation of the mansion. The architects' report read, "It was necessary to reconstruct the interior of the White House from basement to attic, in order to secure comfort, safety and necessary sanitary conditions."

Because the State Dining Room had been too small for entertaining ever since the White House was first built, McKim planned to enlarge it by removing the grand staircase that had been constructed between the State Dining Room and the Family Dining Room, thereby increasing the State Dining Room's seating capacity from about sixty to more than one hundred. A new grand stairway would then be built to the left of the main front door that would descend from the second floor to the Cross Hall opposite the Green Room.

On the second floor the inadequate plumbing and wiring would be replaced and the offices turned into bedrooms or sitting rooms, complete with bathrooms and closets. The wide center hallway would be divided by sliding glass doors into three living areas dominated at either end by the beautiful fan-shaped lunette windows. Up in the attic, one-third of the space would be used for storage, with the rest being turned into servants' rooms, closets and workrooms.

McKim was at his imaginative best in the basement, now to be known as the Ground Floor. Although the basement had been cut up into small workrooms crisscrossed by wires, cut through by heating and plumbing pipes and covered with a hundred years of kitchen grease and whitewash, McKim immediately recognized the beauty of Collen Williamson's "fine, groined arches." Moving the kitchens and service rooms into the west end of the Ground Floor and the West Wing, McKim planned to restore the walls to their original stonework as well as turn the old oval furnace room into a handsome Diplomatic Reception Room which guests could enter from the south side of the house.

Although the East Wing had been demolished years ago, McKim designed a whole new East Wing that would become the social entrance to the White House. Entering by a circular driveway, guests would leave their wraps in a cloak room, walk through a long hallway past reception rooms and offices into the Ground Floor vaulted hallway and up a flight of stairs into the Entrance Hall on the State Floor.

For a cost of $6,000, McKim insisted on tearing down all the greenhouses on the west side of the house that had been multiplying for the past fifty years. Although Roosevelt himself commanded, "Smash the glass houses!" they had traditionally kept the White House supplied with fresh flowers and Mrs. Roosevelt wasn't willing to part with them until she was promised a new greenhouse nearby.

McKim's ingenious plan was to add an Executive Office Building onto the end of the old West Wing that would house all the presidential offices. Because the building would be set back from the front of the White House and constructed on the downside of the slope, it would be hardly noticeable from the street. When Congress appropriated $65,000 for its construction, McKim had planned for "a permanent, adequate, and thoroughly dignified office" to be built later. But after only six months, McKim's "temporary" offices had become permanent.

On the roofs of the one-story East and West wings that would extend out one hundred and sixty feet from the White House, terraces were to be built that could be entered from the State Dining Room on the west and the East Room on the east and used for entertaining in pleasant weather, much as they had been in Jefferson's time.

McKim's plans rearranged, remodeled and reconstructed the White House into what it basically is today, with the family and guest entrances on the north and south, the social entrance through the East Wing and all business callers entering on the west.

When work began in June 1902, McKim wrote, "The house is torn to pieces . . . bedlam let loose does not compare with it." All the woodwork, floors, ceilings, walls, windows and doors were ripped up, leaving much of the interior gutted down to its wooden framing. The floor-to-ceiling stained-glass screen that had been designed by Louis Tiffany in the 1880s that separated the Entrance

Louis Tiffany's ornate stained-glass screen decorated with flags and eagles that separates the Entrance Hall and the Cross Hall is removed during the 1902 renovation.

Hall and the Cross Hall was one of the first victims. Although a White House guest had observed earlier that the screen created "a marvelously rich and gorgeous effect," because McKim wanted to open up the Entrance Hall, the screen had to go, and out it went (and disappeared from all record) to be replaced by six new columns. The ornate hand-wrought iron fence erected on the north side of the house in 1833 during Andrew Jackson's presidency was next on the scrapheap.

The Roosevelts, who were living in nearby Townsend House and not liking it one bit, were anxious to move back in, especially since the White House always opened the Washington social season in December. "Without fail," Roosevelt wrote to McKim, "we must have the last piece of work completed by December first." But that was only six months away!

Because McKim, like all architects working with a White House deadline, was being pressured to hurry (and the Roosevelts were not ones to be kept waiting), much of what he did was superficial instead of structural, such as depending on the old brick inner walls to carry the full weight of steel I-beams on which the new flooring would eventually rest. (Both the Entrance and Cross Hall floors were to be of heavy Joliet stone.) The cutting of lumber was haphazard, with sawdust and bits of wood left between the old second-floor timbers and the new flooring above it, creating a potential fire hazard in the family quarters. Rather than wire mesh and a complete replastering job, some of the ceilings were put up by simply driving in thousands of nails and then covering the nailheads with a thin coat of plaster.

As for decorating, McKim would have preferred all-new furniture for his all-new White House but funds were running out. Because each presidential family had wanted the most modern, up-to-date furnishings over the years, all sorts of worn-out or old-fashioned furniture, chandeliers, carpets, draperies and knick-knacks had either been thrown out or sold at auctions, including the Bellangé furniture that was sold in 1860 (eight pieces of which were returned to the White House more than one hundred years later). The most dramatic cleanup was when Vice President Chester Arthur, who became President after the assassination of James Garfield, arrived at the White House in 1881 and announced, "I will not live in such a house as this."

The following year, President Arthur, known as "Elegant Arthur," auctioned off twenty-four wagonfuls of "decayed furnishings," a record not matched until twenty years later when McKim sold off twenty-six. As great admirers of Lincoln, the Roosevelts at least rescued the Lincoln bed and furniture from the auction block. "I think of Lincoln, shambling, homely, with his strong, sad, deeply-furrowed face, all the time. I see him in the different rooms and in the halls," Roosevelt once said, a remark that may have led to the legend that Lincoln's ghost haunted the mansion. The Roosevelts also saved President Ulysses S. Grant's old Cabinet table, Presidential and First Lady portraits and the pier table purchased by Monroe that turned up in the attic, the only piece of Bellangé furniture that had never left the White House.

In November 1902 the Roosevelts moved back in to face the same plaster dust, smells and chaos that Jefferson had endured in 1801 and Monroe in 1817. And all the construction work had stirred up the mice and rats that had made their home in the White House since 1800. A newspaper article about the problem brought suggestions from all over the country, including a shipment of six white cats from a concerned citizen. In the 1940s the White House housekeeper was still complaining about ants, rats, mice, cockroaches and moths. "We were the testing ground for every new disinfectant," she wrote. Despite decades of efforts, White House rodents continued to make news as late as 1989.

At last, on December 18, 1902, the work was basically finished. Because each incoming President and First Lady had decorated the mansion as they pleased, the American people had always looked upon the White House as an extension of their own homes and taste. But no longer. Although McKim hadn't taken history into account, in a sense he had created history. What the White House (its official name since 1901) had lost in warmth and a certain "hominess," it had gained in dignity and a formal grandeur.

McKim removed all the mantels in the mansion except for the

The East Room, which was elaborately decorated by President Ulysses S. Grant in 1873, meets with architect McKim's disapproval.

two 1817 Monroe marble mantels in the State Dining Room, one of which he installed in the Red Room and one in the Green Room. The East Room, which had been ornately decorated in "steamboat palace Gothic" by President Grant in 1873, had its false ceiling, gilded columns and other Victorian clutter replaced by a look of late 18th-century classic simplicity, with oak parquet flooring, richly carved paneling and three new chandeliers.

With the second floor now given over entirely to living quarters, presidential and staff offices were located in the Executive Office Building. Traditionally called the West Wing, the handsome one-story building with simple lines was faced with painted white brick.

Well pleased with McKim's results, Roosevelt wrote to his son Kermit, "You will be delighted with the White House. The changes have improved it more than you can imagine." Now, with the proper setting, the Republican President and First Lady launched into entertaining on a scale never before seen at the White House, with a social schedule of "private dinners, small dances, musicales, formal luncheons, teas, 'at homes,' receptions and garden parties." It was "a continual two-step and spirited waltz for seven and a half years. The music varied but the pace never ceased," recalled the chief usher. From his office by the north door, the chief usher supervised the entire operation of the White House and its staff in consultation with the President and First Lady, just as the chief usher does to this day.

Although it was true that there could be only one leading man at the White House, the Roosevelt family made a wonderful supporting cast, with an aide describing Edith Roosevelt as having spent her years as First Lady "without ever having made a mistake." (Although Presidents' wives had been called "First Lady of the Land" since the 1870s, the title "First Lady" came into common use during the Roosevelt administration.)

"Princess Alice," Roosevelt's lovely but willful daughter from his first marriage, who refused to go to boarding school, fascinated the nation with her clever retorts, escapades, cigarette smoking, automobile driving and party-going. When he was once asked if he couldn't do something about Alice, Roosevelt replied, "I can be President of the United States or I can control Alice. I cannot possibly do both."

The public, through the ever-present press, also followed the antics of the "White House Gang," the five younger Roosevelt children, their cousins and friends, who roller-skated and bicycled in the East Room, slid down the stairs on trays, transported a pony in the White House elevator, threw spitballs at Andrew Jackson's portrait and owned a collection of badgers, raccoons, ponies, mice, rats, dogs, cats, snakes, parrots and guinea pigs.

"I don't see what good it does *me* for you to be President," Quentin complained when his father scolded him for walking on stilts through a White House flower bed. "A nervous person had no business around the White House in those days. He was sure to be a wreck in a very short time," observed Ike Hoover, who had first worked at the White House as an electrician and remained forty-two years through ten administrations to become chief usher in 1913. Like Ike Hoover, most of the houschold staff stay on from administration to administration, some serving in the White House for ten, twenty or even thirty years.

Life at the Roosevelt White House was strenuous for family and staff alike, with Roosevelt, who was as fun-loving as his children, staging pillow fights, sparring with former heavyweight champion

Archie and Quentin Roosevelt line up with the White House police for an early-morning roll call.

John L. Sullivan and taking jujitsu lessons. "When Theodore attends a wedding, he wants to be the bride, and when he attends a funeral, he wants to be the corpse," a relative once remarked. Roosevelt didn't deny that he was having a good time. "I don't think that any family has ever enjoyed the White House more than we have," he wrote to Kermit.

An observer wisecracked, "You must always remember that the President is about six." But that observer was wrong. Teddy Roosevelt, who had once said, "The White House is a bully pulpit," may have joined in the fun but he was no child. He knew exactly where he stood in relation to America and where America stood in relation to the world. He knew what he wanted to accomplish as President and how he was going to accomplish it.

As the 20th century began, America's new position as a world leader increased demands on both the country and the President. And expectations for the White House had to expand along with expectations for the newly visible nation. The reconstructed and redecorated mansion, which was no longer simply a larger version of Mr. and Mrs. Everyman's private home, had become instead a permanent setting for future Presidents as they stepped into the central theater of action to play out America's new role in the world.

In a dramatic display of American naval power, President Theodore Roosevelt dispatches the sixteen battleships of the Great White Fleet on a fourteen-month cruise around the world.

7 THE WHITE HOUSE IN ISOLATION

THE PRESIDENT AND HIS WIFE left the White House late at night on December 3, 1918, for the short drive to the Washington railroad station. Several hundred onlookers applauded as they boarded the presidential car *Ideal* for the trip to Hoboken, New Jersey, where a transport ship was waiting to take them to France. For the first time in history an American President was traveling to Europe.

At the Hoboken pier early the next morning, the President and First Lady walked briskly between lines of soldiers, passed under a great arch and made their way up the gangplank of the transport *George Washington* as the Navy Band played "Hail to the Chief" and "The Star-Spangled Banner." Two hours later the big ship backed away from the pier to the roar of a 21-gun salute, whistles, sirens, bells, sprays of water and two airplanes performing loop-the-loops overhead. Tens of thousands of well-wishers had gathered along the shorelines as the *George Washington* steamed down the Hudson River and out to sea.

The next day *The New York Times* reported, "President Wilson,

The President and First Lady bid farewell to America as they leave for France and the Peace Conference on the transport ship *George Washington.*

with Mrs. Wilson at his side, stood on the bridge of the great transport and waved his hands and tipped his hat time and time again to show his appreciation of New York's parting tribute."

President Woodrow Wilson, inaugurated on March 4, 1913, was the first American President who considered the concerns of Europe to be the concerns of America as well. Now Wilson was traveling to France for a meeting with other world leaders to draw up terms for a peace treaty after the defeat of Germany in World War I. A born crusader, Wilson had drafted Fourteen Points as a guide for the treaty and he was prepared to fight for those ideals in Paris.

But back home, most Americans weren't interested in the ideals that Woodrow Wilson was willing to fight for. In the period after World War I, which ended in November 1918, the nation was plagued by a shaky economy, skyrocketing prices, shortages, strikes, social unrest, race riots, and militant women demanding the vote (suffragettes). With more than 116,000 American dead and 204,000 wounded in Europe, the American people believed they had sacrificed enough for Europe and they pulled back from any further involvement. And just as the nation withdrew into isolation, so too did the White House. Although President Wilson was personally committed to making the world "safe for democracy," ironically, the Wilson White House became the most isolated White House in history.

Writing almost a hundred years earlier, a longtime Washington resident observed that it was possible for the President to "remain invisible, and as much separated from social intercourse as if on the other side of the mountains." Wilson himself admitted that there was "a very holy and very terrible isolation" in the presidency, but in many ways that was what he wanted. A loner with almost no male companions, Wilson was a devoted family man whose wife, Ellen, and their three daughters were his best friends.

PRESIDENT WILSON IS DECEIVING THE WORLD
WHEN HE APPEARS AS THE PROPHET OF DEMOCRACY

PRESIDENT WILSON HAS OPPOSED THOSE WHO
DEMAND DEMOCRACY FOR THIS COUNTRY

HE IS RESPONSIBLE FOR THE DISFRANCHISEMENT
OF MILLIONS OF AMERICANS

WE IN AMERICA KNOW THIS
THE WORLD WILL FIND HIM OUT.

"I will not permit my home to be used for political purposes," Wilson had announced early in his career and he never did.

Interestingly enough, although Wilson may have appeared aloof in public, his daughter Eleanor remarked that within his family circle, he was "our most amusing and gay companion." His personal doctor, Cary Grayson, agreed, noting that Wilson "cherished privacy. He was never happier than in the bosom of his family, sitting before the fireplace in the Oval Room, chatting comfortably. He would pun, recite nonsense verse and limericks."

But within less than a year, all that changed with the death of Wilson's wife, Ellen, in August 1914 and the marriage of two of his daughters. After losing his wife, a deeply unhappy Wilson wrote to a friend of his "intolerable loneliness and isolation," only overcoming his depression when he met and fell in love with Edith Galt, a Washington widow. Advised that the public would disapprove of a too-early second marriage, Wilson described his view from the

Suffragettes burn fires to keep warm as they picket an unsympathetic President Wilson for seven years until they finally win the right to vote in 1920.

White House, ". . . in this place time is not measured by weeks, or months, or years, but by deep human experiences . . ." He and Edith Galt were married privately in December 1915.

By that time, World War I was raging in Europe and although Wilson tried desperately to keep the United States neutral, on April 6, 1917, he signed a proclamation of war against Germany. Although Presidents Lincoln and McKinley had both tried to maintain as normal a White House as possible during wartime, President Wilson did not. Elizabeth Jaffray, who served as White House housekeeper for fifteen years, later wrote, "The moment war was declared the White House lost all official responsibility. All State dinners and receptions were done away with, the public was barred from the White House grounds, the doors of the Executive Mansion were doubly and trebly guarded, and guards were placed on the top floor." (The White House wasn't opened again to the public until Wilson left office in March 1921.)

The Oval Office, which had been added to the West Wing under President William Howard Taft in 1909 as the first State Room since the White House was built, had been at the center of the presidency ever since. But Wilson preferred to use his second-floor study in the family quarters, where he could work undisturbed, often writing speeches and letters on his own typewriter. "I have found by experience that the only place I can get things done is the White House," he noted. "We are so safely (almost annoyingly) guarded here nowadays that we, as a matter of fact, have a great deal of seclusion and privacy . . ."

Although it was certainly true that staff demands, as well as a constant stream of visitors to the West Wing, slowed down work and interrupted schedules, it was also true that those personal contacts kept the President in touch with people and issues. Wilson, who was not at his best in one to-one meetings, almost never consulted his Cabinet or party leaders, so that the very privacy he longed for in order to think clearly and form his own opinions isolated him even further. With no radio, TV or extensive telephone communication systems, only the press provided feedback and criticism to a President increasingly secluded in the White House.

Wilson, whose favorite relaxation was to cruise on the presidential yacht alone with his wife, wrote to one of his daughters, "Edith and I are on the *Mayflower* today to get away from the madness (it is scarcely less) of Washington for a day or two, not to stop work . . . but to escape *people* and their intolerable excitements and demands."

And then, in November 1918, World War I was over and Wilson announced that he would travel to the Peace Conference in Paris to fight for his Fourteen Points for peace. The most important to Wilson was the fourteenth Point, which would create "A general association of nations" to be called the League of Nations that would enforce world peace and make "forever impossible" another war. "It is to America that the whole world turns to-day," Wilson

President Woodrow Wilson and his second wife, Edith, are seldom apart after their marriage in 1915.

said. "The hungry expect us to feed them, the homeless look to us for shelter, the sick of heart and body depend upon us for cure."

Wilson's advisers were opposed to his going to Paris, believing he had a stronger voice if he directed negotiations from Washington rather than personally tangling with the crafty and worldly-wise European leaders. But there was no keeping Wilson home. His private secretary wrote, "He had supreme confidence in himself and only in himself to secure what he fought for."

Both Theodore Roosevelt and William Howard Taft had traveled to Central America during their terms of office but they had been gone for only brief periods. Now Wilson would be away from the White House from December 3, 1918, until July 8, 1919, with only a one-week return in midwinter to consult with the Senate Foreign Relations Committee. As the White House stood empty and isolated month after month, Americans could hardly be blamed for believing that their President cared more about Europe's problems than their own.

But Wilson had a vision. "Here is the great issue upon which the future peace of the world depends," he told Senate leaders during his brief return in February 1919 as the Peace Conference dragged on. Under the pressure of the very tough negotiations, Wilson's health, which had never been good, worsened, with his associates in Paris describing his appearance as "thin and grey" . . . "utterly worn out" . . . "often one side of his face twitching with nervousness" . . . "a tired old man."

After months of bickering and arguing, which one observer compared to a "riot in a parrot house," Wilson reluctantly agreed to compromise on his first thirteen Points in order to have the fourteenth Point, the League of Nations, written into the Treaty. On June 28, 1919, Wilson, along with thirty-one other national leaders, signed the Treaty of Versailles to officially end World War I. But for the Treaty to be official in the United States, two-thirds of the Senate had to approve, or ratify, its terms.

In July, Wilson arrived back in the United States from Europe so exhausted, his secretary said he was "on the verge of a nervous breakdown." Chief usher Ike Hoover noted that on his return to the

The "Big Four" of the Peace Conference chat on the porch of President Wilson's Paris residence, (left to right) Great Britain's David Lloyd George, Italy's Vittorio Orlando, France's Georges Clemenceau and America's Woodrow Wilson.

White House, the President "was doing a lot of resting, retiring to his room from time to time during the day, shutting himself off from all the world."

Although Wilson was determined to see the Treaty ratified by the Senate, he had been gone a long time and his political power had weakened badly. More to the point, he was out of touch with the widespread sentiment that Americans now wanted only to take care of themselves . . . not the world. It was a time of withdrawal and isolation for an America that was tired of solving other nations' problems.

Nevertheless, Wilson was certain that if he could only reach the people, he could convince them of the Treaty's merits. Despite continued poor health, in August, Wilson announced his decision to travel across the country by train speaking in defense of the Treaty. "Dare we reject it and break the heart of the world?" he asked.

Wilson's family and doctor were strongly opposed, with Dr. Grayson predicting that Wilson was "risking disaster." It didn't matter. "I cannot put my personal safety, my health in the balance against my duty—I must go," Wilson responded.

On September 3, 1919, the President, Mrs. Wilson, Dr. Grayson and their party left the White House and boarded the special train that would eventually take them to twenty-seven cities, where Wilson would make a total of forty speeches. Dr. Grayson later wrote that for Wilson, "the journey was a prolonged period of physical pain; for Mrs. Wilson and me an unceasing agony of anxiety." As the trip progressed, Edith Wilson described how her husband's headaches became so severe "he was almost blind during the attacks." And then on September 25 at Wichita, Kansas, the President collapsed and the train sped back to Washington, ending Woodrow Wilson's personal crusade forever. Although he seemed better for a few days, on October 2 he suffered a massive stroke from which he never fully recovered.

At first the White House denied that Wilson had even had a stroke. "No details, no explanations," was Ike Hoover's curt description of how the public and press were kept in the dark. It wasn't until twenty years later that Edith Wilson admitted, "He had suffered a stroke, paralyzing the left side of his body. An arm and one leg were useless, but, thank God, the brain was clear and untouched . . . Nurses came and the house was organized as a hospital."

A month after Wilson's stroke, Colonel Edward House, Wilson's political adviser, wrote in his diary, "The President's condition is such that no one is seeing him outside of his physician and Mrs. Wilson." Two months later Colonel House noted that "the President is much sicker than the public is led to believe." As Wilson lay totally disabled in the Lincoln bed, the chief doctor told Edith Wilson, "But always keep in mind that every time you take him a new anxiety or problem to excite him, you are turning a knife in an open wound. His nerves are crying out for rest, and any excitement is torture to him."

Mrs. Wilson was determined to protect her husband and by assuming what she called "my stewardship," that was exactly what she did. She later wrote, "I studied every paper, sent from the different Secretaries or Senators, and tried to digest and present in tabloid form the things that, despite my vigilance, had to go to the President. The only decision that was mine was what was important and what was not, and the *very* important decision of when to present matters to my husband."

Although the press and public became increasingly alarmed about "Mrs. President's" powers, she didn't care. "Woodrow Wilson was first my beloved husband whose life I was trying to save, fighting with my back to the wall, after that he was President of the United States."

In numerous memoirs published later, the household staff, who had closer contact with the President than anyone else, described that stressful time. Ike Hoover wrote, "The President was sicker than the world ever knew, and never afterwards was he more than a shadow of his former self." Wilson's Secret Service agent, Ed Starling, observed, "It is true that Mrs. Wilson and Dr. Grayson stood between the President and the rest of the world while he was ill. How much they kept from him will never be known." Housekeeper Jaffray reported, "He was a figure pitiful beyond words."

The deeply concerned Senate sent two senators to the White House to interview Wilson and report back on his condition. Propped up in the Lincoln bed, with his useless left arm under the covers, Wilson managed to get through the brief interview with humor. Republican Senator Albert Fall, who was one of the Democratic President's most outspoken critics, approached the bed. "Well, Mr. President, we have all been praying for you," he said. "Which way, Senator?" was Wilson's quick-witted response.

When Wilson was finally able to get out of bed, he was wheeled around the White House and out on the porch in a large wheelchair. With only an hour or so a day spent in his office, Wilson's time was occupied by watching movies and taking drives in the car.

Woodrow Wilson's appearance at one of his early Cabinet meetings contrasts dramatically with his appearance at a Cabinet meeting after his stroke.

"I feel so weak and useless," he said in March 1920. "I feel that I would like to go back to bed and stay there until I either get well or die."

It wasn't until April 1920, seven months after his collapse, that Wilson met with his Cabinet. "The President looked old, worn, and haggard," wrote his Secretary of the Treasury. "It was enough to make one weep to look at him. One of his arms was useless. In repose, his face looked very much as usual, but, when he tried to speak, there were marked evidences of his trouble. His jaw tended to drop on one side, or seemed to do so. His voice was very weak and strained."

Certainly with the White House totally isolated, the possibility of Wilson's resignation was widely discussed. Only a few days after Wilson had suffered his stroke, Secretary of State Lansing suggested to Wilson's secretary, Joseph Tumulty, that the President should resign. "You may rest assured that while Woodrow Wilson is lying in the White House on the broad of his back I will not be a party to ousting him," Tumulty retorted.

Edith Wilson later recalled that she had discussed her husband's resignation with the chief doctor, who had responded, "For Mr. Wilson to resign would have a bad effect on the country, and a serious effect on our patient."

Wilson himself considered resignation. In April 1920 he said to Dr. Grayson, "My personal pride must not be allowed to stand in the way of my duty to the country. If I am only half efficient I should turn the office over to the Vice-President." But his heart obviously wasn't in the offer, for he later mentioned the possibility of running for a third term.

During the seven months of Wilson's acute illness, the Senate was debating Treaty ratification, and although Wilson's political power was gone and his health was ruined forever, he still refused to approve of any amendments that might have saved the Treaty. *"We must take it without changes which alter its meaning, or leave it,"* he stated. On March 19, 1920, the Treaty was defeated in a final vote of the Senate and with that decision, the United States took a giant step into isolating itself from the rest of the world. (A separate peace treaty with Germany wasn't signed until 1921.)

Woodrow Wilson was a visionary President who had looked into the future and said, "I can predict with absolute certainty that within another generation there will be another world war if the nations of the world do not concert the method by which to prevent it." Wilson, who was awarded the Nobel Peace Prize in December 1920, had been responsible for shipping food and medicine to Europe after World War I that had saved millions of lives. And under his banner of freedom, a number of nations were able to throw off the yoke of oppression.

President Herbert Hoover later wrote about Wilson, with whom he had worked closely, "With his courage and eloquence, he carried a message of hope for the independence of nations, the freedom of men and lasting peace." On the other hand, Hoover also wrote, "Mr. Wilson was completely isolated from the political currents in motion . . . his lack of contact with people and their leaders separated him from the reality of which sound compromises are made." A Cabinet officer perhaps summed up Wilson best, "He was the most extraordinary and complex character I ever encountered."

After Wilson's second term ended in March 1921, America retreated even further into isolation. The 1920s, called the Roaring Twenties, the Gin and Jazz Age and the Dollar Decade, were caught up in bright lights, fast cars, flappers, movie stars, sports heroes, speakeasies and bathtub gin.

And the White House reflected those years of self-interest and isolation. President Warren Harding was elected in 1920 with the slogans "A return to normalcy" and "America First!" followed by President "Silent Cal" Coolidge who advised the country to "Keep Cool with Coolidge," followed in turn by President Herbert Hoover promising continued prosperity with "Two Chickens in Every Pot and a Car in every Garage." Even President Franklin D. Roosevelt's first two terms were concerned with solving the country's overwhelming economic problems.

Although many in America, including President Roosevelt, were troubled by the storm clouds of war gathering over Asia and

Europe, it wasn't until the United States entered World War II in December 1941 that the nation and the White House fully emerged from isolation into a position of world responsibility and commitment.

With a membership of four and a half million in the 1920s, the bigoted Ku Klux Klan stages a parade down Washington's Pennsylvania Avenue.

8 THE WHITE HOUSE AS HOST

THE WHITE HOUSE HAD NEVER SEEN such a dusting, mopping and scrubbing. Old rugs were replaced and draperies were cleaned, floors were waxed and furniture polished. When June 8, 1939, finally arrived, the White House housekeeper, Henrietta Nesbitt, wrote, "If I do say so, the lovely old house shone like a brand-new stove!"

No White House visitors had ever caused such excitement, but then again it wasn't every day that the King and Queen of Great Britain were to be guests of the President and First Lady. For weeks, all sorts of instructions had been arriving at the White House, with Mrs. Nesbitt commenting, "I was being snowed under with advice and menus and suggestions." The King was to be served his food thirty seconds before the Queen, a hot water bottle was to be provided for every bed (despite the June heat), photographers' flashbulbs were not to go off any closer than fifty feet away. Even the President sent out memo after memo. "The King and Queen arrive tomorrow," he worried. "I devoutly hope everything will go through without any upsets."

Top:
Accompanied by a military escort, a formally dressed President and King George VI ride from the railroad station to the White House to begin the British royalty's State visit, June 1939.
Bottom:
Despite her parasol, Queen Elizabeth is sunburned during her drive to the White House with the First Lady in an open limousine.

On June 8, after the President and First Lady had formally welcomed the King and Queen at Washington's railroad station, the official party started off for the White House. Five hundred thousand cheering spectators lined the route as President Franklin D. Roosevelt and King George VI led the procession in one open limousine, with First Lady Eleanor Roosevelt and Queen Elizabeth following in a second.

The 1939 royal visit was no simple social call. This was a state affair planned in every detail for a very definite purpose: to reinforce American and British ties in the face of an increasingly hostile Nazi Germany. Sure enough, less than three months after the King and Queen returned home, World War II exploded in Europe.

Although their Majesties' stay was one of the most memorable in White House history, it wasn't the first time the White House had been host to foreign dignitaries. Beginning in 1805 with Thomas Jefferson's welcome of Native American Indians (considered to be foreigners), the White House had hosted the French Marquis de Lafayette in 1825, envoys from Imperial Japan in 1860, King David Kalakaua of the Sandwich Islands (Hawaii) in 1874 and Prince Henry of Prussia in 1902. Nevertheless, it wasn't until Franklin Roosevelt's administration that a steady stream of visitors began to arrive. Assistant chief usher J. B. West recalled, "For the Roosevelts, the White House was like a Grand Hotel."

With guests invariably arriving with gifts, perhaps no gift has ever been used by so many Presidents as the *Resolute* desk. In 1855, a Yankee whaler had freed the British ship *Resolute* from the Arctic ice and towed her to an American port for repairs. The following year, President Franklin Pierce presented the refitted *Resolute* to Great Britain's Queen Victoria as a gift from the American people. When the *Resolute* was broken up in 1880, the oak timbers were made into a desk that Queen Victoria, in turn, presented to President Rutherford B. Hayes.

Like other Presidents before and since, Franklin Roosevelt used the *Resolute* desk in the Oval Office, the difference being that he seldom left his chair, whether for meetings, appointments or even press conferences. Paralyzed from the hips down as the result of a polio attack in 1921, Roosevelt was able to stand and walk only because his legs were locked into ten-pound braces, and his full weight was supported by a strong aide on one side and a cane on the other.

Despite his handicap, Roosevelt projected such an image of vitality and good health, few were aware of his disability. "Photographers were on their honor not to photograph him in his wheelchair," a newspaperwoman reported. Secret Service agent Ed Starling, who served under five Presidents beginning with Woodrow Wilson, commented about Roosevelt, "Literally thousands who

In 1878 President Rutherford B. Hayes receives the first Chinese diplomats to the United States in the oval Blue Room.

had seen him at ball games, rallies, and inaugurations never suspected his condition."

Roosevelt's physical limitations meant that he had to find alternate means of reaching the people. Housekeeper Nesbitt wrote, "He couldn't go out to them. He asked them in." And one way he accomplished this was by radio. Only eight days after taking office in March 1933, Roosevelt, conscious of the symbolic setting of the White House, broadcast his first fireside chat from the Diplomatic Reception Room to a nation panicked by the worst economic depression in its history.

For the next twelve years, Roosevelt's reassuring voice on the radio established what could only be called a personal relationship with his listeners. Eleanor Roosevelt said of her husband, "His voice lent itself remarkably to radio. It was a natural gift." One of his Cabinet officers remarked that when Roosevelt broadcast to the people, "his face would smile and light up as though he were actually sitting on the front porch or in the parlor with them."

Mrs. Roosevelt, who was Teddy Roosevelt's niece and her husband's distant cousin, had always been concerned with social issues. Now she became the President's "eyes and ears" as she met people and listened to their concerns in "city slums, rural areas, poor mining towns." As Roosevelt launched his New Deal programs that created government jobs for the unemployed and helped the poor with direct relief, he was anxious to hear the public's reaction. "Franklin often used me to get the reflection of other people's thinking," Eleanor wrote and it was true. "My Missus says that people are working for wages way below the minimum set in the town she visited last week" was a typical presidential comment at a Cabinet meeting.

With the Secret Service code name of "Rover," Eleanor traveled constantly, authored a daily newpaper column, wrote books, lectured, made radio broadcasts and was the first President's wife to hold her own press conferences (women reporters only). Assistant chief usher J. B. West later noted, "Contrary to published reports, Eleanor Roosevelt never walked anywhere. She ran." And she had the ability to laugh at herself. In her newspaper column, she told

From the beginning of her husband's presidency, Eleanor Roosevelt plays an active role in such social programs as serving soup to the hungry on a Depression breadline.

about the time she was visiting a prison and the President asked where she was. "She's in prison, Mr. President," came the reply. "I'm not surprised," he quipped. "But what for?"

Although the parents of five grown children, for many years the Roosevelts had lived separate lives. An upstairs maid observed, "The Roosevelts rarely saw each other before dinner time, if then." J. B. West commented, "We never saw Eleanor and Franklin

Roosevelt in the same room alone together. They had the most separate relationship I have ever seen between man and wife. And the most equal."

Certainly they were both equally criticized. As a result of his highly controversial programs, Roosevelt aroused stronger feelings than almost any President who ever served. Eleanor Roosevelt said that her husband was "hated wholeheartedly by some and loved equally wholeheartedly by others."

Because Mrs. Roosevelt herself was so highly visible, she came in for her share of disapproval, too. Other First Ladies had been criticized, Abigail Adams and Sarah Polk for their political influence, Mary Lincoln for her extravagance and her Southern background, Edith Wilson for taking over presidential duties, but none was so widely criticized, and often ridiculed, as Eleanor Roosevelt. "Instead of tearing around the country, I think you should stay at home and personally see that the White House is clean," suggested a letter writer, much to Mrs. Roosevelt's amusement.

Both Roosevelts were not only political Democrats but democrats with a small "d" as well, and in the tradition of Andrew Jackson, they opened the White House to anyone who struck their interest or who had a story to tell. Eleanor Roosevelt wrote, "I love people. I love having people in my home." Minority groups, women, laborers, small-business men, blacks, farmers, movie stars, intellectuals, progressives and thousands of ordinary people were all welcomed in countless numbers. "The world and his wife and his children and his second cousins came to the White House," Mrs. Nesbitt wrote. "One of our biggest troubles around the White House was getting rid of guests," an upstairs maid complained. "Guests would actually be waiting in the hall while previous guests were still packing."

And then with the Japanese attack on Pearl Harbor on December 7, 1941 ("a date which will live in infamy"), everything changed. Because the United States was in danger from aerial attack, the White House was closed to tourists, military patrols guarded the grounds, blackout curtains were hung at every window, the staff was equipped with gas masks, a bomb shelter was built under the White House and the Roosevelt family was more heavily protected than ever. A secret Map Room on the Ground Floor that was conveniently located opposite the elevator was set up with telegraph and telephone lines and guarded around the clock.

Although the Army wanted to paint the White House black, Roosevelt flatly refused. "I never forget that I live in a house owned by all the American people and that I have been given their trust," Roosevelt had said in one of his fireside chats. In that vein, he had a prayer carved into the State Dining Room mantel that John Adams had written in a letter to his wife in 1800 after his first night in the White House. "I Pray Heaven to Bestow the Best of Blessings on THIS HOUSE and All that shall hereafter Inhabit it. May none but Honest and Wise Men ever rule under This Roof."

Having served as President Wilson's Assistant Secretary of the Navy during World War I, Roosevelt knew that the White House could become a guarded fortress in wartime and he was determined not to let his physical disability isolate him the way Wilson had been isolated. He needn't have worried. His secretary described his outgoing nature. "He was interested vitally and actively in people, in places, and in things." And once the United States was at war, Washington and the White House became an ever-more popular destination. "All these world leaders were swooping down on us from all directions," recalled Mrs. Nesbitt.

Soviet Minister for Foreign Affairs V. M. Molotov, who arrived at the White House secretly for a long weekend in 1942, was listed in the guest book simply as "Mr. Brown." Mrs. Roosevelt later wrote, "One of the White House valets was quite astounded when he unpacked Mr. Molotov's bag to find inside a large chunk of black bread, a roll of sausage and a pistol."

Some guests were more difficult than others. Madame Chiang Kai-shek, the wife of the Chinese generalissimo, arrived in 1943 with forty servants and aides for a nine-day visit. Called the Dragon Lady by White House personnel, Mme. Chiang Kai-shek,

President Franklin D. Roosevelt is able to pose standing beside his White House guest Madame Chiang Kai-shek in 1943 only with the support of a military aide and a cane.

who clapped her hands for service and ate most of her meals in her room, demanded that her silk sheets and pillowcases be washed and ironed every time she used them, however briefly.

Certainly Great Britain's Prime Minister Winston Churchill was one of the White House's more strenuous visitors. On December 22, 1941, only two weeks after war was declared, Churchill, who remarked that meeting Roosevelt was like opening a bottle of champagne, arrived in great secrecy. Following his own schedule, Churchill stayed up until two or three A.M., slept until at least noon and often conducted business from his bed. Because he was accustomed to more service than the White House usually provided, extra servants had to be ready to meet his demands for special food, cigars and brandy. Complaining constantly about the heat, Churchill kept changing bedrooms until he finally settled on the Rose Bedroom, now called the Queens' Bedroom in honor of the queens who have stayed there.

On New Year's Day 1942, during the first of Churchill's three wartime visits, a historic document was signed in the White House between the United States, Great Britain, Russia and China that began the process of binding twenty-six countries into a "united nations" (Roosevelt's name for the organization) against Germany, Italy and Japan.

The following year, on November 9, 1943, representatives of forty-four United Nations signed an agreement in the East Room for the United Nations Relief and Rehabilitation Administration. Never had the White House been host to such a large and distin-

British and American chiefs of staff line up behind a seated Prime Minister Winston Churchill and President Roosevelt on the south grounds of the White House in 1943.

guished gathering of foreign leaders brought together for such an important event. Mrs. Roosevelt later commented that her husband "believed in dramatizing special occasions, and he carefully planned that [the signing] be done with pomp and ceremony." And, it might be added, he held the meeting in the White House to emphasize America's commitment to the future of world peace.

The strain of conducting the war as Commander in Chief, traveling extensively for wartime conferences and hosting a constant parade of guests year in and year out was exhausting, and Roosevelt welcomed the new presidential retreat in the Maryland mountains sixty miles from Washington near the Pennsylvania border. Originally a rustic log cabin camp that had been built during the 1930s, the property was converted by the National Park Service for use by the President and his guests (Eleanor Roosevelt seldom went there). Roosevelt's name for the retreat, Shangri-La, meaning *hidden paradise,* was later changed by President Dwight D. Eisenhower to Camp David after his grandson, the name it still carries.

In September 1978, President Jimmy Carter brought together Egypt's President Anwar el-Sadat and Israel's Prime Minister

Anwar el-Sadat smiles his approval as Menachem Begin and Jimmy Carter shake hands after the peace treaty between Egypt and Israel is signed on the south lawn of the White House, March 26, 1979.

Menachem Begin at Camp David which resulted in a historic peace treaty between their two countries called the Camp David accord.

Retreat or no retreat, the twelve years of heavy presidential responsibility through an unprecedented three terms began to take its toll on Roosevelt's health and by 1945, he looked so frail and ill, photographers were requested not to take any close-up pictures. Giving wartime restrictions as his reason, Roosevelt asked that his fourth inauguration be held on the South Portico of the White House rather than at the Capitol. On January 20, 1945, in a steady drizzle, the White House played host to some two thousand guests

The photograph of Franklin Roosevelt's fourth inauguration on the South Portico taken from the Washington Monument gives a bird's-eye view of the White House, its East and West wings and the grounds, known as the President's Park.

as Franklin D. Roosevelt was sworn into office for a fourth term. (In 1933 the Twentieth Amendment to the Constitution had changed the inauguration date from March 4 to January 20.)

The White House had been the setting for only one other inauguration. In 1877, March 4 fell on a Sunday, which automatically postponed the swearing-in ceremony until March 5. But President Ulysses S. Grant, fearing violence after a bitter and hotly contested election, arranged to have the newly elected Rutherford B. Hayes secretly sworn into office in the Red Room during a White House dinner party on March 3, with the traditional ceremony held two days later at the Capitol without incident.

Roosevelt died of a cerebral hemorrhage on April 12, 1945, less than three months after his fourth term began. Two hours later Harry S. Truman became the third President of the United States to be sworn in at the White House, this time in the West Wing Cabinet Room surrounded by Roosevelt's grief-stricken staff.

In the years to come, President Truman, and every President who has followed him, has continued to greet the nation and the world at the White House in the spirit of the Roosevelts. During a six-year period, President Ronald Reagan hosted 94 presidents, 7 kings, 3 queens, 77 prime ministers, 45 foreign ministers, a sheik and 13 princes. Actually, the parade of guests at the White House became so overwhelming, since the mid-1950s most official visitors have stayed at the government-owned Blair House across Pennsylvania Avenue from the White House.

"We have learned to be citizens of the world, members of the human community," Roosevelt had said in his fourth inaugural address, and no matter what new ideals, goals or political philosophies incoming Presidents have brought to the White House, they have all understood that our nation can never again avoid responsibility as the leader and host to the free world. And the White House, as both the President's home and his official seat of power, stands ready to extend a cordial welcome.

Top:
President Dwight Eisenhower and the First Lady pose with Queen Elizabeth II and Prince Philip on the North Portico in 1957, the second generation of British royalty to be State guests at the White House.
Bottom:
In 1985, Prince Charles and Princess Diana, Great Britain's third generation of royalty to visit the White House, chat by the west lunette window with President and Mrs. Reagan.

9 THE WHITE HOUSE REBUILT

THE WHITE HOUSE, OF COURSE, had always had a reputation for ghosts, but the President was from Missouri, the Show-Me state, and he was convinced that the mansion's creakings and groanings were more than just the restless spirits of past Presidents. At a reception in 1947 the President noticed the Blue Room chandelier trembling and swaying, while a few weeks later, he noted in his diary that his study floor "sagged and moved like a ship at sea."

The following year the leg of his daughter's piano sank into the floor. "Margaret's sitting room floor broke in two but didn't fall through the family dining room ceiling," the President wrote. "They propped it up and fixed it. Now my bathroom is about to fall into the red parlor. They won't let me sleep in my bedroom or use the bath."

By November 1948 the President described how a special committee had "found the White House in one terrible shape. There are scaffolds in the East Room, props in the study, my bedroom, Bess's sitting room and the Rose Room . . . We've had to call off all

Blair House is connected to the Blair-Lee House next door to make more comfortable living quarters for the President and his family during the years of White House reconstruction.

functions and will move out as soon as I come back from Key West."

Which is just what they did. By Thanksgiving 1948 President Harry S. Truman, his wife, Bess, and daughter, Margaret, had packed their belongings and moved across Pennsylvania Avenue to Blair House, little guessing that it would be more than three years before they could return to their rightful place in the White House.

When the Trumans arrived at the White House in May 1945, they had found the family quarters shabby and worn-out after wartime neglect and hard use by the large Roosevelt clan. Margaret Truman wrote in her diary, "The White House upstairs is a mess . . . I was so depressed when I saw it." Assistant chief usher J. B. West, who had shown the Trumans around the mansion, noted, "What little was left of the White House gave it the appearance of an abandoned hotel." Still, after almost four years of an all-consuming war, the White House was no shabbier or worn-out than the nation itself.

Then, with the dropping of two atomic bombs over Japan in August 1945, World War II ended and a brand-new era dawned. Servicemen and women returned home to start new jobs or go to college on the GI Bill, rationing books were thrown out, cars rather than tanks rolled off the assembly line and both the baby and the building boom were launched.

As the nation began its postwar recovery, the White House began its own recovery program, with Democratic President Truman declaring, "I'm going to have the most thorough study ever made of every nook and cranny, beam and pipe in the old house." In February 1948 he appointed a blue-ribbon committee of engineers and architects to make a top-to-bottom inspection of a White House that had been the victim of haphazard construction for years.

Mrs. Woodrow Wilson in 1913 had supervised the addition of bathrooms and other conveniences in the attic that so overloaded the third floor, by the 1920s engineers were recommending that

After World War II, GIs everywhere are given a hero's welcome home by their mothers, including Supreme Commander of the Allied Forces in Europe, Dwight D. Eisenhower, whose mother greets him at the Kansas City Airport in 1945.

both the roof and the third floor be replaced. When President Calvin Coolidge was told that the White House roof was unsafe, he joked, "I presume there are plenty of others who would be willing to take the risk of living under that roof."

Nevertheless, in March 1927, the Coolidges had to move out so that construction could begin. Hoban's old slate roof and timber framing were removed, the attic was demolished down to the upper walls of the second floor, a steel frame was constructed, hollow concrete tiles were laid to form the third-floor walls and a new steel roof was put in place. When the work was finished, the old attic had become a full third floor just as Hoban had originally planned it, with fourteen rooms, storage and service areas and a delightful solarium (sun-room) built on the South Portico roof.

In 1929 Herbert Hoover completely remodeled the West Wing and although a fire damaged the building only six months later, it had been rebuilt the following year. President Franklin Roosevelt quietly began an extensive program of remodeling and building in 1933, the same year that the National Park Service took over supervision of the White House. With donations from around the country, a swimming pool for Roosevelt's use was constructed in the basement area that led from the White House to the West Wing.

The West Wing offices were gutted, a two-story basement excavated and the Oval Office moved so that it could be entered from the colonnaded porch without having to enter the West Wing at all. In December 1941, Roosevelt had architect Lorenzo S. Winslow rebuild the interior of the East Wing into a three-floor structure that housed five offices, six rooms, a movie theater and a bomb shelter in the new subbasement.

Even though Roosevelt had also added offices in the space between the West Wing and the new swimming pool, when Truman became President, he suggested another addition, complaining that "the basement of the so-called office wing, is full of workers—it is the poorest place in the world for people to work . . ." But when Lorenzo Winslow, now promoted to White House Architect, mentioned the fatal word "addition," as well as revealing that a West Wing extension would cover a greater area than the White House itself, public outrage doomed Truman's hopes. (Roosevelt had been careful to use words such as "reorganization" and "a few new rooms.")

Recalling pleasant Missouri evenings spent on back porches, an angry but undaunted Truman next suggested a "back porch" for the White House to be located on the second floor behind the columns of the South Portico. The porch, which would be the first exterior change at the White House since 1902, created such an uproar, Margaret Truman commented that her father might just as well have "announced he was going to replace the White House with a lean-to or a split-level bungalow."

Truman, who prided himself on being an "architectural nut," insisted that the porch would not only improve the mansion's appearance but also provide enjoyment for the President and his family. "Of course, I wouldn't expect you to take into consideration the comfort and convenience of the Presidential family in this arrangement," he wrote angrily to the Commission of Fine Arts which had objected to the plan. Although Truman got his porch in 1948, now known as the Truman balcony, opinions about it have remained strong . . . and mixed. "When the job is finished, everyone will like it," Truman had predicted somewhat optimistically. (The backs of twenty-dollar bills had to be redesigned to show the new porch.)

By 1949, Margaret Truman wrote that the special committee of engineers and architects whom her father had appointed had inspected the White House and noted that the mansion "was standing up purely by habit." The repeated cry of hurry-hurry-hurry that had been raised by every President since George Washington had finally caught up with the old building. It was now no longer a question of what Truman wanted or didn't want, it was a question of whether the White House could be saved at all.

The timber that Hoban had used in 1817 for the interior walls and partitions presented a serious fire hazard, but even more importantly, the timber structure could no longer support the weight that it was now carrying. The bell systems, plumbing, heating, water, gas and electrical wires, ducts and pipes that had been cut into wood partitions, supporting beams and the inner brick walls had weakened the building structurally at the same time that they had added weight. McKim in 1902 had run steel beams under the State Rooms and removed a bearing wall to enlarge the State Dining Room, while Coolidge's 1927 steel roof and steel-and-concrete third floor had added such a burden to the floor below, Hoban's old stone walls had begun to shift.

Truman, whose nickname was "Give-'Em-Hell Harry," wrote in his diary, "If Theodore Roosevelt and old man Coolidge had done as they should, we wouldn't be out of doors now! Mr. Kim Meade White [architects] did a botch job in 1902 and the silent? old man from Mass. [Coolidge] did a worse one in 1927. It's hell. None of the Roosevelt tribe gave a damn about the official residence."

In April 1949 a concerned Congress authorized the formation of a six-member Commission on the Renovation of the Executive Mansion, to be appointed by the President. After more study, the Commission offered three possible choices, all drastic: (1) Preserve the outer walls, roof and third floor and gut the interior, (2) Demolish the building but save the outer stone walls for use on a new building, (3) Demolish the entire building and construct a new one.

Despite being the most difficult and expensive solution, it was unanimously decided that the walls, roof and third floor should be saved and the interior gutted. Truman, a history buff, declared, "I'll do anything in my power to keep them from tearing down the White House if only we can get Congress to agree." Congress did agree, voting $5,400,000 for the project. Everyone else involved in the project agreed, too, especially architect Winslow, who was particularly concerned with preserving as much of the historic interior as possible.

After a high protective fence was built around the work site to keep out the curious public, shoring up of the outer stone walls began on December 12, 1949. Although the walls were in reasonably good condition, the clay-and-sand soil on which the White House had originally been founded and which had been so ideal for brickmaking wasn't adequate to support the heavy steel-and-concrete structure that would eventually go up. Fortunately, there was a twenty-foot-thick bed, or stratum, of sand and gravel under the White House at a depth of about twenty-five feet that would provide a reliable footing. Some 126 pits about four feet square were dug in sections directly under the stone walls down to this sand-and-gravel stratum. Concrete was then poured into the pits to create piers that would support the stone walls.

When the dismantling of the interior began on December 13, 1949, Winslow numbered and crated as much of the woodwork and mantelpieces as he could, but the old wood was so dry, most of it cracked and split. About all the woodwork that Winslow was able to save was the second-floor structural timber that was later used to panel some of the Ground Floor rooms.

Those materials that weren't to be used again were labeled "surplus" by the commission and donated to interested institutions or government agencies, made into kits for sale to the public or simply disposed of, mostly for landfill. Because preservation of old materials took time and manpower, much of the flooring, window and door trim, mantelpieces, chair rails, baseboards and doors was simply sent out gutted windows and down wooden chutes to be hauled away. For twenty-two straight days, caravans of trucks carted off discarded materials for resale or landfill. Meanwhile, Winslow arranged to have the old moldings and cornices measured and cast

With all the doors and windows boarded up, debris from the second and third floors of the White House is sent down chutes for disposal.

in plaster for reproduction before they were removed, one of the most time-consuming jobs on the project.

Before demolition of the floors and partitions could begin, temporary steel columns had to be installed to support the outer stone walls, the heavy roof and the third-floor framing. Large holes were cut in all the floors so the temporary steel columns could extend from the subbasement to the third floor. Steel crossbeams and diagonal bracing rods were then fastened between the temporary columns to add stability.

One of Hoban's old brick walls is visible from the second-floor oval room.

With the outer walls, roof and third floor securely supported, excavation of a new two-story basement could begin. Because Truman wouldn't allow any opening cut in the original stone walls, a disassembled bulldozer was taken into the ground-floor level through a door and reassembled inside. The bulldozer then excavated a wide passageway underneath the stone walls through which more heavy equipment could enter to start the excavation.

On February 14, 1950, construction of a permanent structural steel frame was begun at the same time that the interior walls, partitions and floors were being removed. Because all the work had to be accomplished inside the stone walls, which would now carry only their own dead weight, most of the eight hundred tons of structural steel had to be brought into the house through the windows! With the freestanding steel frame eventually bearing all the weight of the house and everything in it, the steel columns were securely founded on piers of reinforced concrete (concrete reinforced with steel rods) that had been sunk into the sand-and-gravel stratum. To avoid any possible error when removing the temporary columns, the permanent columns were painted a different color.

By the fall of 1950 the gutted White House was such an awesome sight, photographs of the interior weren't released for fear of public reaction. The huge hollow shell, 168 feet long, 85 feet wide, 60 feet high on the north and 70 feet high on the south, was crisscrossed from top to bottom by steel framing, with the original walls now visible from the inside. President Truman, a longtime member of the Masonic order, found the chisel marks left by Collen Williamson's 18th-century stonemasons of particular interest.

Now the old familiar cry of hurry-hurry-hurry was raised once again. In June 1950 the Korean War had broken out, creating shortages of both labor and materials and causing prices to soar, all of which resulted in deadlines coming and going without being met. As the Cold War with Russia became increasingly "hot," military advisers and the Secret Service convinced Truman that the subbasements should be bombproof, adding extra time and cost to the project.

After the reinforced concrete floors had been laid by pouring

In preparation for
excavating, by June 1950,
heavy equipment is
already inside the White
House, now only an
empty shell supported by
temporary steelwork.

concrete on a steel wire bedding, the interior partitions were installed on the ground-, first- and second-floor levels. In order for the dimensions of the State Rooms to remain the same, modern heating, plumbing, air conditioning, electrical and communications systems, not to mention the heavy steel frame, had to be precisely fitted into spaces that had been designed long before any such conveniences were known.

Some three hundred workers were on the job by the fall of 1951

A permanent steel beam is maneuvered through a window in the Family Dining Room.

Hoban's vaulted Ground Floor ceiling has already been reproduced, but the marble facing for the floor and walls has yet to be finished.

Carpenters install the lunette window at the east end of the family quarters.

as wooden floors were laid over the concrete flooring, paneling was put up and chandeliers and lighting fixtures were repaired and rewired. Although endless delays held up work on the marble grand stairway and new marble mantels, eight new Doric columns of Vermont marble and a new marble floor were installed in the Entrance Hall (Winslow had been unable to save the 1902 Joliet stone floor). Window sashes went up and doors were hung, with eighteen painters working inside the house throughout the winter of 1951–2. The steps and floors of both North and South porticoes were replaced, while the exterior of the White House was completely repainted.

As decisions were made concerning lighting, wallpaper and colors, President Truman, who had been an outspoken "sidewalk superintendent" throughout construction, increasingly voiced his always-strong opinions. Meanwhile, interior designers, working with what funds were left over, were frantically decorating under the direction of the hardworking commission, with the colors of the State Rooms, of course, remaining traditional.

And then in March 1952, the work was finished for a final cost of $5,761,000. As with every White House building project, the carpentry sheds, electrical and cabinet shops, offices and other construction shacks were torn down, the scaffolding was removed, the landscaping was replaced and the commissioners made a tour of the house before the President and his family moved back in. The commissioners were well pleased with the mansion that was the same and yet different, historic and yet new. Like most engineering projects, the most difficult and costly part of the project, the structural framework and mechanical equipment, was hidden beneath and within the familiar stone walls and interior.

After Truman made his own inspection tour on March 2, he wrote in his diary, "I spent the evening going over the house. With all the trouble and worry it is worth it—but not 5 ½ million dollars! If I could have had charge of the construction it would have been done for half the money and in half the time!"

In addition to vaults under the north driveway in which air-conditioning equipment and electrical machinery were located, the two basements housed the service rooms, storage areas, carpenters' and plumbers' shops, as well as the heating and ventilating systems. The Ground Floor layout remained the same, with the old kitchen under the Entrance Hall re-created with stone arches and two huge fireplaces and the groin-vaulted hall reproduced with marble facing. Leading off the central hall were the Library (begun under First Lady Abigail Fillmore in 1851), Map Room, oval Diplomatic Reception Room and China Room, where the china collections of past Presidents are displayed.

The only major change on the State Floor was the design of McKim's grand staircase, which Truman had always disliked as being too steep and narrow. Now the staircase descended gradually from the second floor to a series of landings that ended in the Entrance Hall instead of the Cross Hall. At either end of the State Floor were mezzanine levels built out of sight between the first and second floors which housed service areas, the chief usher's office and rest rooms for guests. Truman expressed an interest in keeping Teddy Roosevelt's old elevator but as he reported later, "I wanted

The Trumans return to
the reconstructed White
House at 6:20 P.M. on
March 27, 1952.

to get that old bird cage back in here, but they told me you couldn't get modern elevator works in with it."

On the second floor, the family rooms remained basically the same except for better closet space and more conveniently located bathrooms. The long central hall on the second floor was divided by great arches into three sitting-room areas, with Hoban's handsome lunette windows reproduced at either end.

When the Trumans moved back into the White House on March 27, 1952, the President was presented with a gold key. "The contractor who remodeled the White House gave me a gold master key to all the Yale locks. It opened all of them [the locks] tonight but the one I wanted to get into," Truman wryly noted in his diary.

The White House household staff was delighted to welcome back the presidential family whom they affectionately called "The

Three Musketeers." J. B. West wrote, "The Trumans were the closest family who lived in the White House during the twenty-eight years I worked there." Perhaps one of the reasons for the Trumans' popularity was their genuine interest and concern for the people who staffed the mansion. A military aide wrote about Truman, "He spoke to everybody as he walked through—the gardeners, the painters, and had something to say about what was going on."

Although on the surface, the newly finished White House appeared much as it always had, it now had 132 rooms, including service and utility rooms, as compared to the original thirty-six. During that time, the nation had also grown, from thirteen states with a population of some four million in 1792 to forty-eight states populated by over 150 million in 1952.

Over those same years, the grounds had seen changes, too. The original White House property had covered sixty acres that included what is now Lafayette Park on the north down to Tiber Creek (filled in during Monroe's administration) on the south. Beginning with John Quincy Adams's museum of trees and plants, there have been almost as many different gardens and landscapes as there have been Presidents. The south grounds have been used for award ceremonies, press conferences, concerts, military reviews, picnics, Easter egg rolling, a playground, putting green, croquet court, exercise yard, horseshoe pit and helicopter pad, not to mention a pasture for a small flock of sheep which kept the lawn cropped during World War I.

But more than growth and numbers have changed. With the splitting of the atom in the 1940s, the nation entered a new technological age that has witnessed a computerized society developing nuclear energy, satellite telecommunications and space exploration. And the White House has kept pace. As a modern, fireproof institutional complex equipped with the latest technological improvements, Abigail Adams's prediction in 1800 that "this House is built for ages to come" had at last come true.

President George Bush gets some exercise by pitching horseshoes on the south lawn.

10 THE WHITE HOUSE ON-CAMERA

ALTHOUGH THE COMMENTATOR of the 1962 TV special wasn't a professional, she was given star treatment. But then again the commentator was the First Lady and the special was to be a televised tour of the White House. The crew, who had to work around the private life of the First Family as well as thousands of tourists a week, was also concerned about their heavy equipment possibly damaging the historic house. Early on in the filming everyone was horrified at the sound of a terrible crash as a light tower was being moved through the Cross Hall with its two-hundred-year-old chandeliers.

"See if it's ours or theirs," the producer managed to order.

With what must have been great relief, he reported, "It was ours: a large light bulb had fallen out of a reflector."

During the hour-long program, the First Lady recounted historical events and pointed out objects of interest in the State and Ground Floor rooms. At the end of the show, the First Lady and the show's host, Charles Collingwood, were joined by the President, who observed, "Anything which dramatizes the great story of the

The television camera focuses on the First Lady as she enters the East Room behind the handsome piano presented to the White House by Steinway & Sons in 1938.

United States—as I think the White House does—is worthy of the closest attention and respect by Americans who live here and who visit here and who are part of our citizenry."

With Mr. Collingwood's thank-you, "A Tour of the White House with Mrs. John F. Kennedy" concluded.

Jacqueline Kennedy's TV special in February 1962 awakened great public interest in the mansion as a national treasure. "Everything in the White House must have a reason for being there," Mrs. Kennedy said, and with that goal in mind, she supervised the formation of two White House commissions under a permanent curator to oversee donations and purchases of furnishings and paintings, a program that has been continued by every administration since.

Although President Truman had taken the nation on a TV tour of the rebuilt White House in 1952, the program had been more like a home video than the professional production with Mrs. Kennedy just ten years later. But in the early 1950s, television was still in its infancy. Only 11 percent of American families owned television sets in 1950, while by 1960 that number had soared to 88 percent.

In 1960, when presidential candidates John F. Kennedy and Richard Nixon held four televised debates, television itself played a key role in deciding who would next occupy the White House. According to polls taken later, those listening to the debates on the radio declared that the candidates were about even, while those watching on TV rated Kennedy ahead in three out of the four debates.

In the first debate, Vice President Nixon, who had refused to wear makeup, appeared so thin, nervous and sweaty, his mother had phoned in after the program to ask if he was "feeling all right." Nixon later noted, "What hurt me the most in the first debate was not the substance of the encounter between Kennedy and me, but the disadvantageous contrast in our physical appearance." After

In the early days of television, very small screens are installed in very large sets.

winning the 1960 election, the less well-known Kennedy, who had come across as a vital, self-assured and appealing young candidate, admitted, "It was TV more than anything else that turned the tide."

Only three years later, when President Kennedy was assassinated on November 22, 1963, television again played a major White House role. Just as the funeral train carrying Abraham Lincoln's body from Washington to Illinois allowed the country to participate in the mourning process for Lincoln, so television allowed the country to participate in the mourning process for Kennedy. A social scientist, recalling how a grief-stricken nation was riveted to its TV sets for four days, wrote, "I stayed before the set, knowing—as millions knew—that I must give myself over entirely to an appalling tragedy."

Kennedy's funeral, deliberately planned to resemble Lincoln's, witnessed the White House draped in black, the East Room viewing (Kennedy's casket was closed), six white horses, the riderless horse with the boots reversed, the procession moving out from the North Portico to the slow and measured pace of muffled drums and the lying-in-state in the Capitol Rotunda on Lincoln's catafalque to allow the public to pay its last respects. One of the most astonishing

John F. Kennedy's coffin leaves the White House on the same caisson that carried Franklin D. Roosevelt's coffin in 1945.

scenes ever televised took place on November 24 when the President's accused killer, Lee Harvey Oswald, was shot to death in front of millions of stunned witnesses.

Kennedy's assassination was followed by the 1968 assassinations of Senator Robert F. Kennedy and Dr. Martin Luther King, Jr., two attempts on President Gerald Ford's life in 1975 and the serious wounding of President Ronald Reagan in 1981. With a seemingly endless display of violence showing on the home screen, many believe that television has to take some responsibility for the increasing violence in American society. "In no nation on earth is shooting people made so glamorously attractive by the media," an ABC journalist has commented.

The media, of course, were a presence at the White House long before television. For most of the 19th century, journalists had simply "hung around" the White House recording the comings and goings of visitors, trying to pin down Presidents for an interview and in general getting news from where and from whom they could. With the 1902 reconstruction of the White House, reporters at last had their own small press room in the new West Wing. "Newspapermen nowadays have access to the President," a Washington newspaper announced. "Thus the White House has become a regular assignment for reporters."

In 1969 Franklin Roosevelt's old swimming pool was covered over to create a new Press Lobby with two floors of booths for writers and broadcasters and a briefing room where the some two hundred reporters and photographers who regularly cover the White House are briefed daily.

Although Teddy Roosevelt was the first President to hold press conferences, Franklin Roosevelt was the first to allow himself to be quoted directly, while Dwight D. Eisenhower was the first to have his press conferences televised (they were taped for later cutting and editing). Eisenhower, who was known for his somewhat garbled speech patterns, also allowed newspapers to transcribe his press conferences. "This decision made a number of people nervous," he later wrote. "A word-for-word transcription, of course, seldom reads like a polished text."

Kennedy began the practice of having his press conferences televised live, although with journalists competing frantically to be called on by the President for a question, it has sometimes been difficult to distinguish the star from the supporting cast. Larry Speakes, Ronald Reagan's press secretary for six years, commented, "The television reporters tend to dominate both the press briefings and Reagan's press conferences . . . the careers of television reporters often could rise or fall on their performance at a press conference."

Because a President's ratings can also rise and fall on his performance, press conferences entail an enormous amount of preparation. In rehearsing Ronald Reagan, Larry Speakes described how even the setting was reproduced, with "a presidential podium, television-type lighting, a microphone, a public address system, and three or four of us at a table, acting as reporters and asking questions . . . We would fire questions, we would follow up, and we would try to trap him; we would try to play the exact role of the press."

With the First Amendment to the Constitution guaranteeing freedom of the press, it goes without saying that Presidents and the media have been traditional adversaries. Probably most Presidents, at one time or another, would agree with Richard Nixon's remark, "I knew that as President my relations with the media would be at best an uneasy truce." Summing up that relationship, Speakes wrote, "In my six years as White House spokesman, it was Us against Them."

Almost two hundred years ago, a newspaper editorial predicted that if Thomas Jefferson was elected President, "Murder, robbery, rape, adultery and incest will be openly taught and practiced." Abraham Lincoln was one of the most vilified of all Presidents, with a New York City newspaper calling him "the great ghoul of the White House" and Southern newspapers describing him as everything from "the Baboon President" to "a low-bred obscene clown."

Ever since Dolley Madison's famous "Wednesday drawing rooms," the media have been almost as concerned with life inside the White House as they have been with the President's political views. During Grant's administration, a Philadelphia newspaper, perhaps speaking for past, present and future media, justified its fascination with the White House. "It is public. It belongs to the people . . . Whoever goes to a levee at the Mansion becomes public property."

The first time that reporters actively pursued a First Family was in 1886 when President Grover Cleveland and his young bride were married in the East Room in the most publicized wedding of the century. On the Clevelands' honeymoon, "the dirty gang," as Cleveland called reporters, camped out nearby, followed the couple with cameras and spyglasses, sprang out of the bushes at them and generally made their life miserable. Media-obsession with the President and his family had begun.

"One of the principal personages of the White House" was how a White House doorkeeper described President Benjamin Harrison's grandson Baby McKee, who was endlessly photographed driving his goat cart around the grounds. Teddy Roosevelt's children were also press darlings, with the chief usher commenting, "Every little event concerning the family, from the highest to the lowest, was broadcast through the newspapers." Sixty years later, the young Kennedy family was equally photographed and quoted, with Caroline Kennedy enchanting the country with her reply to reporters who asked what her father was doing. "Oh, he's upstairs with his shoes and socks off not doing anything."

Lincoln, who was photographed so many times he could right-

While his father tries to work, John F. Kennedy, Jr., peeks out from what he calls "my house," the historic *Resolute* desk.

fully be called the first media President, was well aware of the media's influence on the American people. "What the public believes about the White House and its occupants is indispensable to the strength of the Presidency," he said. ". . . public sentiment is everything. With public sentiment nothing can fail: without it nothing can succeed."

Although the media of Lincoln's time were limited to print, with the advent of radio, instant communication between the President and the American public became suddenly possible. Calvin Coolidge may have made the first nationwide presidential address on radio in 1925, but it was Franklin Roosevelt who perfected the medium as his melodious voice soothed a panicked public during the Great Depression of the '30s and the war years of the '40s. (The Diplomatic Reception Room from which Roosevelt broadcast his fireside chats had only a fake fireplace until a wall was knocked out in 1935 and one of Hoban's original fireplaces was uncovered.)

The dawning of the television age had an even greater impact than radio on the occupants of the White House. Known as the

President Franklin Roosevelt broadcasts a fireside chat to millions of listeners in 1938 from the Diplomatic Reception Room.

"Great Communicator," Ronald Reagan, who had been developing his skills as a radio broadcaster, movie actor and television performer since the 1930s, was probably better prepared to face the ever-present White House TV cameras than any President before or since. His chief of staff observed, "Roosevelt was to radio what Reagan is to television—the first President to master the medium and be defined by it."

On his return by helicopter from Camp David, President Ronald Reagan, accompanied by the First Lady, pauses for a moment to answer media questions.

Lyndon B. Johnson ponders the overwhelming problems of the Vietnam War in the Oval Office.

During the Vietnam War, Lyndon Johnson tried to use television to reassure America the same way that Roosevelt had used radio during World War II. But the Vietnam War, unlike World War II, had deeply divided the country into Doves (those seeking to end the war) and Hawks (those backing the war). In the end, television, rather than working for Johnson, worked against him as the grisly sights and sounds of war were shown nightly on network news. Reporting, whether print, film, radio or television, has always been a subjective profession and TV personnel, who can cut and edit as they choose, were increasingly opposed to the war, a point of view that couldn't help but be reflected in their programming. '

Meanwhile, across the country and up to the very gates of the White House, protesters were televised marching, shouting and picketing against the increasingly unpopular "living room" war. Johnson, barricaded in the White House, at last could hold out no longer and on March 31, 1968, he appeared on national television from the Oval Office. "This country's ultimate strength lies in the unity of our people. There is a division in the American house," he declared. "Accordingly, I shall not seek, and I will not accept the

A sober President Johnson is televised in the Oval Office announcing his decision not to run for a second term, March 31, 1968.

nomination of my party, for another term as your President."

Only six years later, the media brought down another President. This time two *Washington Post* reporters were convinced there was a connection between the June 1972 break-in at Democratic National Committee headquarters and the White House. Although President Nixon's press secretary dismissed the break-in at the Watergate complex as a "third-rate burglary attempt," as more evidence of a "cover-up" came to light, the barricades at the White House again went up.

But when televised hearings of the Senate Watergate Committee began in May 1973 and continued day after day, week after week, into 1974, more Americans became aware of the inner workings of their government than perhaps ever before. And when presidential tapes revealed that Nixon had discussed the cover-up with his staff only six *days* after the Watergate break-in, contrary to his official statement that he hadn't learned of the cover-up until six months after the break-in, impeachment seemed so certain, he was left with little choice. "I shall resign the presidency effective at noon tomorrow," Nixon announced on television from the Oval Office on August 8, 1974, the first presidential resignation in history.

As television established an intimacy between the White House and the American people, the public has been invited into the White House for happy events too: the signing of landmark civil rights legislation, presidential meetings with world leaders, the Egypt-Israeli peace treaty, a TV tour of the family quarters, royal visits, award ceremonies, receptions, parades and weddings. In July 1969 millions of viewers around the world witnessed President Nixon, televised live from the White House, talking by radio-telephone with astronauts Armstrong and Aldrin, televised live from the moon. A continuing series of concerts and programs in the East Room entitled "In Performance at the White House," which was begun under President Jimmy Carter, has been televised for showing on public television. "Jimmy and I knew there were so many people who had never been to the White House," First Lady Rosalynn Carter explained. "We wanted all America to enjoy the White House like we did."

Whether or not one believes that television is the "vast waste-land" that it was first called in 1961, the fact remains that the communications revolution begun in the 1950s has transformed America into a visual and visible nation. Today it isn't even within the realm of possibility that a President could be isolated in the White House for months at a time as Woodrow Wilson was, any more than John Quincy Adams would be able to take a daily swim in the Potomac River without a battery of TV cameras recording the event.

In 1801 President Thomas Jefferson first opened the White House to a handful of people. Today, thanks to television, the White House has become familiar to millions of Americans, making it more than ever what Andrew Jackson first called it, the People's House. Teddy Roosevelt, in his 1903 report to Congress, stated, "The White House is the property of the nation . . . It is a good thing to preserve such buildings as historic monuments which keep alive our sense of continuity with our nation's past."

While escorting a State guest on a tour of the White House, President George Bush used much the same wording as Jackson and Roosevelt: "I want you to see a little touch of our democracy. This house is the people's house. Let's not go in the elevator. At this time of day there are tourists. I don't know who they are, but I'll guarantee you they're from all over our country . . . We're talking about the people's house, and a continuity."

That "continuity" in the "people's house" has reflected this country's good times and bad from 1792 to the present. George Washington, the only President who never lived in the White House, stated that he wanted a building that would look "beyond the present day." And it has. One hundred and sixty years later, President Eisenhower confirmed that George Washington's dream had been realized. "The White House is not just a well-run home for the Chief Executive," Eisenhower wrote. "It is a living story of past pioneering, struggles, wars, innovations and a growing America." As that living story, the ever-changing and yet ever-changeless White House remains today where it has always been, at the symbolic heart of our nation.

Saddened staff members line the South Portico and the Truman balcony as President and Mrs. Richard Nixon bid farewell to Vice President and Mrs. Gerald Ford two hours before President Nixon's resignation takes effect, August 9, 1974.

PRESIDENTS

George Washington [1732–1799]
April 30, 1789–March 3, 1797

John Adams [1735–1826]
March 4, 1797–March 3, 1801

Thomas Jefferson [1743–1826]
March 4, 1801–March 3, 1809

James Madison [1751–1836]
March 4, 1809–March 3, 1817

James Monroe [1758–1831]
March 4, 1817–March 3, 1825

John Quincy Adams [1767–1848]
March 4, 1825–March 3, 1829

Andrew Jackson [1767–1845]
March 4, 1829–March 3, 1837

Martin Van Buren [1782–1862]
March 4, 1837–March 3, 1841

William Henry Harrison [1773–1841]
March 4, 1841–April 4, 1841

John Tyler [1790–1862]
April 6, 1841–March 3, 1845

James K. Polk [1795–1849]
March 4, 1845–March 3, 1849

Zachary Taylor [1784–1850]
March 5, 1849–July 9, 1850

Millard Fillmore [1800–1874]
July 10, 1850–March 3, 1853

Franklin Pierce [1804–1869]
March 4, 1853–March 3, 1857

James Buchanan [1791–1868]
March 4, 1857–March 3, 1861

Abraham Lincoln [1809–1865]
March 4, 1861–April 15, 1865

Andrew Johnson [1808–1875]
April 15, 1865–March 3, 1869

Ulysses S. Grant [1822–1885]
March 4, 1869–March 3, 1877

Rutherford B. Hayes [1822–1893]
March 3, 1877–March 3, 1881

James A. Garfield [1831–1881]
March 4, 1881–Sept. 19, 1881

Chester A. Arthur [1830–1886]
Sept. 20, 1881–March 3, 1885

Grover Cleveland [1837–1908]
March 4, 1885–March 3, 1889

Benjamin Harrison [1833–1901]
March 4, 1889–March 3, 1893

Grover Cleveland [1837–1908]
March 4, 1893–March 3, 1897

William McKinley [1843–1901]
March 4, 1897–Sept. 14, 1901

Theodore Roosevelt [1858–1919]
Sept. 14, 1901–March 3, 1909

William H. Taft [1857–1930]
March 4, 1909–March 3, 1913

Woodrow Wilson [1856–1924]
March 4, 1913–March 3, 1921

Warren G. Harding [1865–1923]
March 4, 1921–Aug. 2, 1923

Calvin Coolidge [1872–1933]
Aug. 3, 1923–March 3, 1929

Herbert Hoover [1874–1964]
March 4, 1929–March 3, 1933

Franklin D. Roosevelt [1882–1945]
March 4, 1933–April 12, 1945

Harry S. Truman [1884–1972]
April 12, 1945–Jan. 20, 1953

Dwight D. Eisenhower [1890–1969]
Jan. 20, 1953–Jan. 20, 1961

John F. Kennedy [1917–1963]
Jan. 20, 1961–Nov. 22, 1963

Lyndon B. Johnson [1908–1973]
Nov. 22, 1963–Jan. 20, 1969

Richard M. Nixon [1913–   ]
Jan. 20, 1969–Aug. 9, 1974

Gerald R. Ford [1913–   ]
Aug. 9, 1974–Jan. 20, 1977

Jimmy Carter [1924–   ]
Jan. 20, 1977–Jan. 20, 1981

Ronald Reagan [1911–   ]
Jan. 20, 1981–Jan. 20, 1989

George Bush [1924–   ]
Jan. 20, 1989–

BIBLIOGRAPHY

Aikman, Lonelle. *The Living White House.* Washington, D.C.: White House Historical Association, 1987.

Ames, Mary Clemmer. *Life and Scenes in the National Capital.* Hartford, Connecticut: A.D. Worthington & Co., 1874.

Andrist, Ralph K. *Andrew Jackson: Soldier and Statesman.* New York: American Heritage Publishing Co., 1963.

———, ed. *The Founding Fathers: George Washington: A Biography in His Own Words.* Vol. 2. New York: Newsweek, 1972.

Annals of the Congress of the United States First Congress. Vol. II. Washington, D.C.: Gales and Seaton, 1834.

Archer, Jules. *World Citizen: Woodrow Wilson.* New York: Julian Messner, 1967.

Athearn, Robert G. *The American Heritage New Illustrated History of the United States.* New York: Dell Publishing Co., 1963.

Baker, Abby G. "The White House of the Twentieth Century." *The Independent,* Vol. LV, No. 2864, October 22, 1903, pp. 2497ff.

Barber, James David. *The Presidential Character.* Englewood Cliffs, New Jersey: Prentice-Hall, 1972.

Barnard, Ella K. *Dorothy Payne, Quakeress.* Philadelphia: Ferris & Leach, 1909.

Bowen, Ezra, ed. *This Fabulous Century.* Vol. VI (1950–1960), VII (1960–1970). Alexandria, Virginia: Time-Life Books Inc., 1987.

Brant, Irving. *James Madison, Commander in Chief 1812–1836.* Vol. 6. Indianapolis: The Bobbs-Merrill Company, 1961.

Brooks, Noah. *Washington in Lincoln's Time.* Edited by Herbert Mitgang. New York: Rinehart & Company, 1895.

Butterfield, Roger. *The American Past.* New York: Simon and Schuster, 1966.

Cable, Mary. *The Avenue of the Presidents.* Boston: Houghton Mifflin Company, 1969.

Caemmerer, H.P.W. *The National Capital.* Washington, D.C.: United States Government Printing Office, 1932.

Chitwood, Oliver Perry. *John Tyler, Champion of the Old South.* New York: D. Appleton-Century Company, 1939.

Colman, Edna M. *Seventy-five Years of White House Gossip.* Garden City, New York: Doubleday, Page & Company, 1925.

Crook, Colonel W.H. *Memories of the White House.* Boston: Little, Brown, and Company, 1911.

Cutts, Lucia Beverly. *Memoirs and Letters of Dolley Madison.* Boston: Houghton, Mifflin and Company, 1887.

Daniels, Josephus. *The Wilson Era: Years of War and After, 1917–1923.* Chapel Hill, North Carolina: The University of North Carolina Press, 1946.

Dos Passos, John. *The Shackles of Power.* New York: Doubleday & Co., 1966.

Eisenhower, Dwight D. *Mandate for Change: 1953–1956.* Garden City, New York: Doubleday & Co., 1963.

The End of a Presidency. Staff of *The New York Times.* New York: Holt, Rinehart and Winston, 1974.

Ferrell, Robert H., ed. *Dear Bess: The Letters from Harry to Bess Truman, 1910–1959.* New York: W. W. Norton & Company, 1983.

————. *Off the Record: The Private Papers of Harry S. Truman.* New York: Harper & Row, Publishers, 1980.

Fields, Alonzo. *My 21 Years in the White House.* New York: Coward-McCann, Inc., 1960.

Fitzpatrick, John C., ed. *Writings of George Washington from the Original Manuscript Sources 1745–1799.* Vols. 31, 32, 34, 35. Washington, D.C.: United States Government Printing Office, 1939.

Flexner, James Thomas. *George Washington and the New Nation (1783–1793).* Boston: Little, Brown and Company, 1969.

Four Days: The Historical Record of the Death of President Kennedy. United Press International and *American Heritage* Magazine. New York: American Heritage Publishing Co., 1964.

Freedman, Russell. *Lincoln: A Photobiography.* New York: Clarion Books, 1987.

Freeman, Douglas Southall. *George Washington, A Biography.* Vol. 6, "Patriot and President," Vol. 7, "First in Peace." New York: Charles Scribner's Sons, 1954.

Freidel, Frank B., Jr. *Our Country's Presidents.* Washington, D.C.: National Geographic Society, 1966.

Furman, Bess. *White House Profile.* Indianapolis: The Bobbs-Merrill Company, 1951.

Garraty, John A. *Woodrow Wilson: A Great Life in Brief.* New York: Alfred A. Knopf, 1956.

Gilman, Daniel C. *James Monroe, 1776 to 1826.* Boston: Houghton, Mifflin and Company, 1890.

Gobright, L.A. *Recollection of Men and Things at Washington.* Philadelphia: Claxton, Remsen & Haffelfinger, 1869.

Grayson, Rear Admiral Cary. *Woodrow Wilson: An Intimate Memoir.* New York: Holt, Rinehart and Winston, 1960.

Green, Constance M. *Washington, Village and Capital.* Princeton, New Jersey: Princeton University Press, 1962.

Green, James A. *William Henry Harrison: His Life and Times.* Richmond, Virginia: Gararett and Massie Incorporated, 1941.

Hall, Florence Howe. *Social Usages at Washington.* New York: Harper & Brothers Publishers, 1906.

Helm, Edith Benham. *The Captains and the Kings.* New York: G.P. Putnam's Sons, 1954.

Hersey, John. "Mr. President: Ghosts in the White House." *New Yorker,* Vol. XXVII, No. 11, April 28, 1951, pp. 36ff.

Hoover, Herbert. *The Ordeal of Woodrow Wilson.* New York: McGraw-Hill Book Company, 1958.

Hoover, Irwin H. *Forty-Two Years in the White House.* Boston: Houghton Mifflin Company, 1934.

Hunt, Gaillard. *Life in America One Hundred Years Ago.* New York: Harper & Brothers Publishers, 1914.

——, ed. *The First Forty Years of Washington Society Portrayed by the Family Letters of Mrs. Samuel Harrison Smith (Margaret Bayard).* New York: Charles Scribner's Sons, 1906.

Hurd, Charles. *Washington Cavalcade.* New York: E.P. Dutton & Co., 1948.

——. *The White House Story.* New York: Hawthorn Books, 1966.

Huth, Hans. "The White House Furniture." *Gazette Des Beaux-Arts,* 6th Series, Vol. XXIX, New York, January 1946, pp. 23ff.

Jackson, Donald, and Dorothy Twohig, eds. *The Diaries of George Washington.* Vol. VI. Charlottesville, Virginia: University Press of Virginia, 1979.

Jacobsen, Hugh Newell, ed. *A Guide to the Architecture of Washington, D.C.* The American Institute of Architects. New York: Frederick A. Praeger, Publishers, 1965.

Jaffray, Elizabeth. *Secrets of the White House.* New York: Cosmopolitan Book Corporation, 1926.

Janson, Charles William. *The Stranger in America.* New York: The Press of the Pioneers, 1935 (published 1807).

Jensen, Amy LaFollette. *The White House and Its Thirty-Five Families.* New York: McGraw-Hill Book Company, 1965.

Kearns, Doris. *Lyndon Johnson and the American Dream.* New York: Harper & Row, Publishers, 1976.

Keckley, Elizabeth. *Behind the Scenes; or Thirty Years a Slave and Four Years in the White House.* New York: G. W. Carleton & Co., Publishers, 1868.

Ketcham, Ralph. *James Madison, A Biography.* New York: The Macmillan Company, 1971.

Kimball, Fiske. "The Genesis of the White House." *The Century,* Vol. 95, No. 4, Feb. 1918, pp. 523ff.

Kunhardt, Dorothy, and Philip Kunhardt. *Twenty Days.* San Bernardino, California: Borgo Press, 1965.

Lash, Joseph P. *Eleanor and Franklin.* New York: W.W. Norton & Company, 1971.

Leish, Kenneth W., ed. *The American Heritage Pictorial History of the Presidents of the United States.* Vols. 1, 2. New York: American Heritage Publishing Co., 1968.

——. *The White House.* New York: Newsweek, 1972.

Lewis, Ethel. *The White House.* New York: Dodd, Mead & Company, 1937.

Lowe, Carl, ed. *Television and American Culture.* Vol. 53, No. 2. New York: The H.W. Wilson Company, 1981.

Marschall, Rick. *The History of Television*. New York: W.H. Smith Publishers Inc., 1986.

Nesbitt, Henrietta. *White House Diary*. Garden City, New York: Doubleday & Co., 1948.

Nixon, Richard. *The Memoirs of Richard Nixon*. New York: Grosset & Dunlap, 1978.

Padover, Saul K., ed. *Thomas Jefferson and the National Capital*. Washington, D.C.: United States Government Printing Office, 1946.

Pendel, Thomas F. *Thirty-six Years in the White House*. Washington, D.C.: Neale Publishing Company, 1902.

Peterson, Merrill E., ed. *The Founding Fathers: James Madison: A Biography in His Own Words*. New York: Newsweek, 1974.

Poen, Monte M., ed. *Strictly Personal and Confidential: The Letters Harry Truman Never Mailed*. Boston: Little, Brown and Company, 1982.

Poore, Ben Perley. *Perley's Reminescences of Sixty Years in the National Metropolis*. 2 volumes. Philadelphia: Hubbard Brothers, Publishers, 1886.

Records of the Columbia Historical Society. "The Writings of George Washington Relating to the National Capital." Vol. 17. Washington, D.C.: Columbia Historical Society, 1914.

Remini, Robert V. *Andrew Jackson and the Course of Freedom 1822–1832*. Vols. II, III. New York: Harper & Row, Publishers, 1981.

Report of the Commission on the Renovation of the Executive Mansion. Compiled under Direction of the Commission by Edwin Bateman Morris, 1952.

Rogers, Lillian Parks, and Frances S. Leighton. *It Was Fun Working at the White House*. New York: Fleet Press Corp., 1969.

————. *My Thirty Years Backstairs at the White House*. New York: Fleet Publishing Corp., 1961.

————. *The Roosevelts: A Family in Turmoil*. Englewood Cliffs, New Jersey: Prentice-Hall, 1981.

Roosevelt, Eleanor. *This I Remember*. New York: Harper & Brothers, 1949.

Roosevelt, Elliot, and James Brough. *A Rendezvous with Destiny*. New York: G.P. Putnam's Sons, 1975.

Rosenbaum, Samuel I. *Working with Roosevelt*. New York: DaCapo Press, 1972.

Ryan, William, and Desmond Guiness. *The White House: An Architectural History*. New York: McGraw-Hill Book Company, 1980.

Sandburg, Carl. *Abraham Lincoln: The War Years*. Vol. 4. New York: Harcourt, Brace & Company, 1939.

Schlesinger, Arthur M., Jr. *The Age of Jackson*. Boston: Little, Brown and Company, 1945.

Seale, William. *The President's House: A History*. Vols. I, II. Washington, D.C.: White House Historical Association, 1986.

Searcher, Victor. *The Farewell to Lincoln*. New York: Abingdon Press, 1965.

Sherwood, Robert E. *Roosevelt and Hopkins*. New York: Harper & Brothers, 1948.

Sidey, Hugh. "The Presidency." *Time,* Vol. 133, No. 22, May 29, 1989, p.24.

Sinclair, David F. "The Monarchial Manners of the White House." *Harper's Weekly,* Vol III, No. 2686, June 13, 1908, pp. 14ff.

Singleton, Esther. *The Story of the White House.* Vols. 1, 2. New York: Benjamin Blom, 1907.

Speakes, Larry, with Robert Pack. *Speaking Out.* New York: Charles Scribner's Sons, 1988.

Starling, Edmund W. *Starling of the White House.* New York: Simon and Schuster, 1946.

Truman, Margaret. *Bess W. Truman.* New York: Macmillan Publishing Company, 1986.

————. *Harry S. Truman.* New York: William Morrow & Company, 1973.

Tuchman, Barbara W. "Woodrow Wilson on Freud's Couch," *Practicing History.* New York: Alfred A. Knopf, 1981.

Tucker, Glenn. *Poltroons and Patriots, A Popular Account of the War of 1812.* Vol. II. Indianapolis: The Bobbs-Merrill Company, 1954.

Tully, Grace. *F.D.R.: My Boss.* New York: Charles Scribner's Sons, 1949.

Tumulty, Joseph P. *Woodrow Wilson as I Know Him.* Garden City, New York: Doubleday, Page & Company, 1921.

Webb, Terrell D. *Washington Wife: Journal of Ellen Maury Slayden from 1897–1919,* New York, Harper & Row, Publishers, 1962.

West, J. B., with Mary Lynn Kotz. *Upstairs at the White House.* New York: Coward, McCann & Geohagen, 1973.

The White House: An Historic Guide. Washington, D.C.: White House Historical Association, 1962.

White House History. Washington, D.C.: White House Historical Association, 1983.

White, Theodore H. *The Making of the President 1960.* New York: Atheneum Publishers, 1961.

Wilson, Edith Bolling. *My Memoir.* Indianapolis: The Bobbs-Merrill Company, 1939.

Wolff, Perry. *A Tour of the White House with Mrs. John F. Kennedy.* New York: Doubleday & Co., 1962.

INDEX

Note: page numbers in *italics* refer to illustrations

CREDITS

Map on p. 12 and White House floor plan on p. 20 by Anita Karl and James Kemp

Photos
The Anne S. K. Brown Military Collection, Brown University: pp. 36, 75
Jimmy Carter Library: p. 114
Century Magazine, September 1912: p. 60
Collection of the City of New York: p. 44
DAR Museum: p. 57
Dwight D. Eisenhower Library: p. 117 (top)
Frank Leslie's Illustrated Newspaper, March 21, 1863: p. 65; March 16, 1889: p. 76
Hall of History, General Electric: p. 136
Harper's Weekly, March 17, 1877: frontispiece; May 6, 1865: p. 62
Lyndon Baines Johnson Library: p. 144 (top and bottom)
John Fitzgerald Kennedy Library: pp. 138, 141
Library of Congress: pp. 17, 26, 38, 40, 47, 50, 54, 58, 67, 68, 70, 73, 74, 79, 82, 87, 88, 95, 97, 100 (top and bottom), 103, 104 (top), 107, 118
Maryland Historical Society: p. 18
National Archives: pp. 15, 33, 90, 93, 109, 112, 113, 115, 121, 134
National Archives, Office of Presidential Libraries: pp. 117 (bottom), 143
National Archives, Nixon Presidential Materials Project: p. 146
National Gallery of Art: p. 16
National Park Service: p. 85
National Park Service, Abbie Rowe Photograph: pp. 125, 126, 128, 129, 130 (top and bottom), 132
Phelps Stokes Collection, New York Public Library: pp. 28, 46
Franklin D. Roosevelt Library: pp. 104 (bottom), 142
Virginia Historical Society: p. 31
The White House, Photograph by Richard Cheek: p. 22
The White House, Photograph by Joyce C. Naltchayan: p. 21
The White House, Photograph by David Valdez: p. 133
The White House Historical Association; Photograph by the National Geographic Society: pp. 2–3